NIETZSCHE
FOR THE 21ST CENTURY

NIETZSCHE
FOR THE
21ST CENTURY

Rebekah S. Peery

Algora Publishing
New York

Library of Congress Cataloging-in-Publication Data —

Peery, Rebekah S.
  Nietzsche for the 21st century / Rebekah S. Peery.
     p. cm.
  Includes bibliographical references and index.
  ISBN 978-0-87586-765-6 (trade paper: alk. paper) — ISBN 978-0-87586-
766-3 (cased: alk. paper) 1. Nietzsche, Friedrich Wilhelm, 1844-1900, I. Title. II.
Title: Nietzsche for the twenty-first century and beyond.
  B3317.P4285 2010
  193—dc22
                              2009051526

Front cover: Friedrich Wilhelm Nietzche, (1844-1900). © Bettmann/CORBIS

Printed in the United States

To Pat and Sandy

TABLE OF CONTENTS

INTRODUCTION

The book which follows is intended to probe once again, to engage in a searching, exploratory, penetrating investigation of the legacy of this 19th century German philosopher. Nietzsche believed that he was giving to the world a gift — not of money, but of his very personal property. He believed, and hoped, that what he had produced or created, his bequest for the future, would grow, would increase in value over time. This legacy would be discovered, or rediscovered, revealing the wealth of his thinking, and the uses, or opportunities, to which this wealth might lead.

During his lifetime (1844–1900) the impact of Nietzsche's thinking was dimly perceived, if at all, by most of his contemporaries or readers. Into and during the 20th century, however, the unexpected, the dangers, but mostly the possibilities, of his ideas began to be recognized, explored, and adopted — and resisted. There were exciting creative achievements far beyond Nietzsche's philosophy. These ideas continued to rapidly display their increasingly amazing and untapped resources.

Well into the 21st century appreciating, interpreting, and evaluating Nietzsche's thinking appear to be rising — still, or again. And he repays generously every effort, every investment.

Nietzsche's task, his mission, as he perceived it, was to challenge, to rethink, redefine, reinterpret, reconceptualize, revalue, any or all ideas — especially those traditional ideas which he increasingly came to believe were important in having the effects of stultifying any process of enhancing or enriching human life — the world we are continually creating and recreating. He sought to change the world by reinterpreting, and perhaps persuading, even propagandizing, others to his cause.

Nietzsche, as we would expect, rejected any notion of repeating traditional models of a system, or systematic philosophizing. Instead, his ideas gradually formed a network — "an intricate pattern or structure suggestive of something woven; or a web of shifting interwoven strands." Or, perhaps better, his thinking was more suggestive of being organic — "having the characteristics of an organism; developing in the manner of a living plant or animal."

My task, as I perceive it, is to identify, or reidentify, those ideas of Nietzsche's which appear to have continually demanded his attention and development. And not only to identify, but also to refocus, to sharpen, put under the microscope, those ideas again — for our time. The fruitfulness and exciting possibilities in Nietzsche's thinking are alive and becoming more enticing. I have become persuaded that the stalk — "the supporting or connecting part; the main stem, often with dependent parts," — the idea which we probably should attend to first, is the idea of *change*.

Nietzsche believed that the world of human beings — always in the process of changing — could be changed, could become something better than it was. That this required changing the ways in which we perceive, feel, and think about this world. That it was his "destiny" to be a major agent of this change. And that his "message" — his new, creative ideas, his words — would someday be heard and understood.

Part One

Suppose, then, that we take as the basic, essential, fundamental aspect of our world — natural and cultural — not space, or time, or bodies in motion, or the four elements, or opposites, or power, or conflict — but *change*. It is present everywhere, or in many places simultaneously — ubiquitous. It is immediately and constantly encountered, present to the senses and to the mind. It is the ground of all of our experiences — both of the outer world and of our inner world. We are placed into this situation, this place, this position, this state, this condition, this relation, at the very beginning. "Thrown into it," as Martin Heidegger might say, "a world which is already going."

Not surprisingly, the idea and the word "change," reflecting, or representing, the phenomenon itself, occur in the form of both a verb and a noun. As a verb, change may mean — "to make different in some particular, to alter; to make radically different, to transform; to give a different position, course, or direction to; to replace with another; to make a shift from one to another, to switch; to undergo a modification; to become different; to pass from one phase to another (as the moon); to undergo transformation, transition, or substitution." As a noun, change may mean — "the act, process, or result of changing; alteration (as in the weather); transformation; substitution (as of scenery); the passage of the moon from one monthly revolution to another; also the passage of the moon from one phase to another."

Look also at the closely related idea or word "process," which may mean — "something going on; a natural phenomenon marked by gradual changes that lead to a particular result (as the process of growth); a natural continuing activity or function (as the process of breathing); a continuous operation or treatment (as the process of producing, of reading, of writing)."

Change, process, and with Nietzsche, *becoming*. Becoming may mean — "any process of change." In traditional philosophical literature, the term had usually referred to Aristotle's formulation of any change involving realization of potentialities. With important expanding applications, Nietzsche focused on the notion of becoming, an important change. He renamed change, gave change a new name, a new sense.

Nietzsche clearly was aware of the importance of the power and significance of the process of *naming*. He wrote these words:

> *Only as creators!* — This has given me the greatest trouble and still does: to realize that what things *are called* is incomparably more important than what they are. The reputation, name, and appearance, the usual measure and weight of a thing, what it counts for — originally almost always wrong and arbitrary, thrown over things like a dress and altogether foreign to their nature and even to their skin –all this grows from generation unto generation, merely because people believe in it, until it gradually grows to be part of the thing and turns into its very body. What at first was appearance becomes in the end, almost invariably, the essence and is effective as such. How foolish it would be to suppose that one only needs to point out this origin and this misty shroud of delusion in order to *destroy* the world that counts for real, so-called "*reality*." We can destroy only as creators. — But let us not forget this either: it is enough to create new names and estimations and probabilities in order to create in the long run new "things." (*GS*,121,122)

With a thinker who recognized the potentialities and powers of ideas, and especially of words, we expect his writings to be abundant with words with different possible meanings, and meanings that were modified in the process of changing the word. This word *becoming* is perhaps one of the most important, although there are countless others.

Naming and renaming, defining and redefining, interpreting and reinterpreting, as Nietzsche was aware, are exercises of power, the power of words. Nietzsche names the universe, and man — the *will to power*:

> And do you know what 'the world' is to me? Shall I show it to you in my mirror? This world: a monster of energy, without beginning, without end; an immovable, brazen enormity of energy, which does not grow bigger or smaller, which does not expend itself but only transforms itself; as a whole of unalterable size, a household without expenses or losses, but likewise without increase or income; enclosed by 'nothingness' as by a boundary; not something flowing away or squandering itself, not something endlessly extended, but as a definite quantity of energy set in a definite space and not a space that might be 'empty' here or there, but rather as energy throughout, as a play of energies and waves of energy at the same time one and many, increasing here and at the same time decreasing there; a sea of energies flowing and rushing together, eternally moving, eternally flooding back, with tremendous years of recurrence, with an ebb and flow of its forms; out of the simplest forms striving towards the most complex, out of the stillest, most rigid, coldest form towards the hottest, most turbulent, most self-contradictory, and then out of this abundance returning home to the simple, out of the play of contradiction back to the joy of unison, still affirming itself in the uniformity of its courses and its years, blessing itself as that which must return eternally, as a becoming that knows no repletion, no satiety, no weariness — : this is my *Dionysian* world of the eternally self-creative, the eternally self-destructive, this mystery-world of the twofold delight, this is my 'beyond good and evil', without aim, unless the joy of the circle is itself an aim; without will, unless a ring feeling goodwill towards itself — do you want a *name* for this world? A *solution* for all your riddles? A *light* for you too, you best concealed, strongest, least dismayed, most midnight men? — *This world is the will to power — and nothing beside!* And you yourself are also this will to power — and nothing beside! (N,136)

It is important to note something to which we will return later. Nietzsche renamed, redefined, reinterpreted *morality*:

— morality understood as the doctrine of the rank-relations that produce the phenomenon we call "life." — (*BGE*,22)

And on the basis of this definition, Nietzsche then became, and named himself, an "immoralist." Much more about this later.

He redefined good, bad, and happiness:

'What is good? — All that heightens the feeling of power, the will to power, power itself in man. What is bad?—All that proceeds from weakness. What is happiness? — The feeling that power *increases* — that a resistance is overcome'. (*N*,76)

These words, change and process, with Nietzsche's wisdom and cleverness became *becoming*. This sense of change, or process, probably was suggested to Nietzsche by his familiarity with the pre-Socratic philosopher, Heraclitus — reported to have observed that wet becomes dry, or hot becomes cold, or sickness becomes health. And, of course, the reverse of the process also occurred.

In the history of ideas in the West, Heraclitus is probably the first recognized person to claim, on the basis of evidence in nature, that the world should be understood in terms of the *eternal process of change*. Of course, we know that he is famous for — and certainly influenced Nietzsche — the idea of the *Logos*. The world is made up throughout with pairs of opposites — in Heraclitus' view — constantly in conflict, but necessarily interdependent. The extant fragments of Heraclitus' writings support our saying that his interpretation of the universe specified together the eternal pattern or order — the Logos — and the eternal process of change. Heraclitus also suggests that the process of change is measured. Excessive abuse is always a stimulus for correction, or restraint. Also, from Heraclitus, three suggestions which influenced Nietzsche's interpretation of change as it refers to an individual person — character determines one's destiny; evil is to be understood as lack of understanding the Logos; and, wisdom is best understood as knowing the Logos, or Rationale. Heraclitus was the early philosopher of *process* and *order*, especially as these are unavoidably obvious in our natural world.

Aristotle's important interpretation of change focused on the distinction between potentiality and actuality. The acorn is, or has, the potential to become the actual oak tree. The acorn develops, grows, changes. For all living substances — similarity of process, repetitive and cyclical, an orderly process established in nature.

Nietzsche's predecessor by only a few decades, the German philosopher, G.W.F. Hegel (1770–1831), suggested sweeping changes when he devoted his attention to *thinking* as a process, and to *history* as a process. Hegel interpreted the process of change involved in thinking — usually referred to as dialectic — as a process in which a concept, or idea, passes over into and is preserved and fulfilled by its opposite. This appears as a modification, or adaptation, of Heraclitus and his observations in nature that wet becomes dry, or hot becomes cold, or sickness becomes health. Hegel was concerned with thinking wet and then thinking dry, thinking hot and then thinking cold. And then thinking the necessary unity of opposites, or contraries. One perceives wet changing to dry, or hot changing to cold. One may think wet changing to dry, etc. Hegel's interpretation of the process of history will be considered later.

Following Hegel's important salvo, in quick order, three major figures carried forward Hegel's new approach to the process of change. The English naturalist Charles Darwin (1809–1882), the Swiss philologist and cultural historian J.J. Bachofen (1815–1887), and the German philosopher Karl Marx (1818–1883). All three owed much to Hegel's original ideas, and all three — but especially Bachofen — were significant in the intellectual environment into which Nietzsche was cast. All four of these forerunners of Nietzsche will figure in our interpretation in some future context. Here it is appropriate, in discussing the idea of change, to remind that the term evolve, or *evolution*, is tied closely to Darwin's theories. Evolution usually may mean "a process of change in a certain direction; a process of continuous change from a lower, simpler, or worse to a higher, more complex, or better state; a process of gradual and relatively peaceful social, political, and economic advance; the historical development of a biological group (as a race or species)."

It is not irrelevant to mention that the notion of change as *revolution* has been suggested as applicable to the theories of all five — Hegel, Darwin, Bachofen, Marx, and Nietzsche. Revolution may mean — "a sudden, radical, or complete change; a fundamental change in political organization; activity or movement designed to effect fundamental changes in the socio-economic situation; a fundamental change in the way of thinking or visualizing something; a change of paradigm (the Copernican Revolution)."

As for Nietzsche, I believe it is possible to claim that he thought that not only is the process of change *eternal*, but that it is *everywhere*, it involves *everything*. Names, meanings, bodies, perspectives, interpretations, experiences, ideas, thoughts, beliefs, opinions, emotions, desires, aversions, interests, wishes, hopes, tastes, powers, strategies, tactics, relations, values — these are a few of the major ones.

Also, and most innovative, exciting, and enticing, was Nietzsche's choice of *becoming* and of the applications that he selected as being important to him, and for us. The development of his thinking about becoming appears to have revealed itself particularly in two of his later writings — in *Thus Spoke Zarathustra*, and in *Ecce Homo*.

This idea of change as becoming appears to have crystallized in the circumstances within which Nietzsche began writing, and wrote *Thus Spoke Zarathustra*. This book, among them all, seems to have been for him the most exciting, and he insisted that it was his greatest achievement. In Chapter Two of Zarathustra's Prologue, this:

> "Zarathustra has changed, Zarathustra has become a child, Zarathustra is an awakened one; what do you now want among the sleepers?" (Z,11)

Shortly following, the first of Zarathustra's Speeches, "On the Three Metamorphoses," reads:

> Of three metamorphoses of the spirit I tell you: how the spirit becomes a camel; and the camel, a lion; and the lion, finally a child. (Z,25)

Most readers of Nietzsche's are aware of, and perplexed as well as delighted by, the vast range of verbal wit that is so characteristic of his writing. One cannot resist his ability to relate seemingly disparate things so as to illuminate or amuse. He relishes metaphors, analogies, puns, puzzles, parables, riddles, symbols, images, allegories, double entendres, irony, and more. The above speech, as is most of this book, is a prime example.

Metamorphosis may mean —"a change of physical form, structure, or substance, especially by supernatural means; striking alteration in appearance, character, or circumstances; marked and more or less abrupt development or change in the form or structure of an animal (a butterfly or frog) occurring subsequent to birth or hatching." Spirit may mean — "a disposition of mind or outlook; intelligent or sentient part of a human being; inclination, impulse, tendency of a specific kind; special attitude or frame of mind; an attitude, or principle, that animates or pervades thought, feeling, or action (spirit of revenge)." Zeitgeist may mean — "spirit of the time; general characteristics of a particular period." Spirit was a prominent word in most of Nietzsche's writings.

In Nietzsche's use or application of his extensive sense of becoming, it becomes clearer that his primary interest and focus is on the single human being, the individual person. Where others were directing their efforts on thinking as such, or on the human species, or on history — biological or cultural — of humans collectively, Nietzsche saw the single human individual as the proper, and most important, subject of study. And it becomes increasingly clearer that he was taking himself and *his own experiences* as his starting point. How might we gain insight into the process of becoming as it infuses every human life?

If the person Zarathustra is considered as a persona of Nietzsche's, then Nietzsche, in his unique treatment, is presenting something of his own stream of consciousness, or his own journey of discovery — his own becoming. I think one could say that whereas Darwin, for example, was exploring the biological evolution of the species, Nietzsche was exploring the psychological, or spiritual, evolution, the process of becoming of the individual. And that means the physical, intellectual, moral, cultural, social process.

In that first of many speeches by Zarathustra, the spirit of the camel is the spirit that would "bear much," that "kneels down, wanting to be well loaded." It is the spirit of acceptance, of humility, of humbling oneself. It is the spirit, in one sense, of "Yes." With the second metamorphosis, the spirit "becomes a lion who would conquer his freedom and be master in his own desert. Here he seeks out his last master: he wants to fight him and his last god." It is the spirit, in one sense, of "No."

My interpretation of this first speech by Zarathustra is this. In speaking about the "spirit," Nietzsche was referring to two situations, or processes. He is using the spirit to mean "the general intellectual, moral, and cultural climate of an era" — the zeitgeist. The recounting of a very lengthy, historical process of his culture — from a long period of merely accepting the intellectual and moral doctrines — "kneeling down like a camel wanting to be well loaded." Wanting what was most difficult. Probably referring to the long reign of Christian ideas and morality, of which Nietzsche had become unabashedly critical. Perhaps he was reminded of Hegel's "conventional citizen," the person who is subject to traditional, conventional morality. And perhaps Nietzsche saw himself in the role of Hegel's "courageous person," that individual who can transcend this traditional morality of his culture and act on the basis of a morality grounded in subjectivity. Following Zarathustra, from that of the camel, had emerged the next cultural, or perhaps, individual spirit, symbolized by the lion. Nietzsche was experiencing a growing vocal resistance to, and rejection of, this spirit of unquestioning acceptance and obedience. The spirit which would be free, "master in his own desert." Nietzsche was living, thinking, writing during the early stages of a turbulent, disruptive, unpredictable threatening cultural era — the magnitude of which he could only sense. And he clearly sensed that this process — from saying "yes" to saying "no" — would eventually, and necessarily, be followed by yet another metamorphosis. And he was perhaps offering a new starting — the spirit of the child.

Nietzsche was speaking of his cultural environment, and at the same time about himself as a person within that process. He had first become a camel, then he had become a lion, and finally a child. Remember, "Zarathustra has changed, Zarathustra has become a child."

Nietzsche here had already become convinced that the greatest challenge, the overwhelming task facing humanity, was to create *new values*, to abandon and destroy old values. His interpretation of the origin of values, how values come into existence, how some person, some action, some thing, *becomes* valuable, had been clearly stated earlier in *The Gay Science*, and should be reiterated frequently:

> We who think and feel at the same time are those who really continually *fashion* something that had not been there before: the whole eternally growing world of valuations, colors, accents, perspectives, scales, affirmations, and negations.
> . . Whatever has value in our world does not have value in itself, according to its nature — nature is always value-less, but has been given value at some time, as a present — and it was *we* who gave and bestowed it. Only we have created the world *that concerns man!* But precisely this knowledge we lack, and when we occasionally catch it for a fleeting moment we always forget it again immediately; we fail to recognize our best power and underestimate ourselves, the contemplatives, just a little. We are *neither as proud nor as happy* as we might be. (GS,241,242)

Later in his writing, when Nietzsche is becoming more focused on values, and particularly on moral values, he writes this important distinction:

> It is obvious that the moral value-characteristics are first applied to *people* and only later, in a transferred sense, to *acts*. This is why it is a sad mistake when moral historians begin with questions like "Why was the compassionate act praised?" (BGE,203)

Nietzsche had changed, was continuing to change. He was waiting, anticipating, the wider cultural changes, which must come, which would come. In that first speech Zarathustra continues:

To create new values —that even the lion cannot do; but the creation of freedom for oneself for new creations — that is within the power of the lion. The creation of freedom for one-self and a sacred "No" even to duty — for that, my brothers, the lion is needed. To assume the right to new values — that is the most terrifying assumption for a reverent spirit that would bear much. Verily, to him it is preying, and a matter for a beast of prey. He once loved "thou shalt" as most sacred: now he must find illusion and caprice even in the most sacred, that freedom from his love may become his prey: the lion is needed for such prey.

But say, my brothers, what can the child do that even the lion could not do? Why must the preying lion still become a child? The child is innocence and forgetting, a new beginning, a game, a self-propelled wheel, a first movement, a sacred "Yes." For the game of creation, my brothers, a sacred "Yes" is need-ed: the spirit now wills his own will, and he who had been lost to the world now conquers his own world.

Of three metamorphoses of the spirit I have told you: how the spirit became a camel; and the camel, a lion; and the lion, fi-nally, a child. (Z,27)

In other places in his writings Nietzsche has suggested that the child is self-centered, always speaks what is seen in its own self-in-terest, and therefore unable to speak dishonestly. And I would add at least this — the child is natural, simple, hears and creates stories.

Among the countless readings of Zarathustra that have been made in the past, or might be made in the future, this I think may be said. It is Nietzsche's personal record of his own struggle and adventures — in unprecedented and inimitable form and language — in coming to what he calls "the highest formula of affirmation that can possibly be attained." It truly is his "Drunken Song." It is his celebration of his own *becoming*, of having reached his ultimate view of life, and of him-self — his "spirits." And of his desire and need to transmit to others this sense of joy, this Dionysian exuberance, this unequivocal "Yes."

PART TWO

The writing of *Thus Spoke Zarathustra* was followed quickly by Nietzsche's *Beyond Good and Evil*, *On the Genealogy of Morals*, *Twilight of the Idols*, *The Anti-Christ*, and *Ecce Homo*, his last. In trying to grasp more fully Nietzsche's notion of *becoming* as fundamental to understanding the development of the individual person, *Ecce Homo* is like nothing else in Western literature. As is true of *Zarathustra*, each one is top of the list in its uniqueness. One look at the full title should leave no doubt as to the relevance of this book for our consideration. The full title is *Ecce Homo: How One Becomes What One Is*. I believe we are fully justified in exploring with care this second personal record, and I anticipate, or expect, rich rewards. As Heraclitus is reported to have said, "If one does not expect the unexpected one will not find it, for it is not reached by search or trail." Perhaps Heraclitus, and Nietzsche, would advise listening instead, paying close attention to his words. While Nietzsche considered *Zarathustra* his greatest gift to mankind, his legacy, I am considering *Ecce Homo* as perhaps his greatest gift of personal property — his last will and testament, his *legacy*.

The book itself is brief, and Nietzsche, I believe, would have presupposed that the reader's familiarity with his earlier works was perhaps an essential prerequisite for appreciating, interpreting, and evaluating this "last testament." However, that being unlikely, my intention is to dare to choose selectively some of those words which I think may highlight this personal record — Nietzsche's telling of his own experiences of becoming "what he had become."

From the beginning — from the Foreword:

> SEEING that I must shortly approach mankind with the heaviest demand that has ever been made on it, it seems to me indispensable to say *who I am*. This ought really to be known already: for I have not neglected to 'bear witness' about myself. But the disparity between the greatness of my task and the *smallness* of my contemporaries has found expression in the fact that I have been neither heard nor even so much as seen. I live on my own credit, it is perhaps merely a prejudice that I am alive at all? ... I need only to talk with any of the 'cultured people' who come to the Ober-Engadin in the summer to convince myself that I am *not* alive... Under these circumstances there exists a duty against which my habit, even more the pride of my instincts revolts, namely to say: *Listen to me! for I am thus and thus. Do not, above all, confound me with what I am not!*

> I am, for example, absolutely not a bogey-man, not a moral-monster — I am even an antithetical nature to the species of man hitherto honoured as virtuous. Between ourselves, it seems to me that precisely this constitutes part of my pride. I am a disciple of the philosopher Dionysos, I prefer to be even a satyr rather than a saint. But you have only to read this writing. Perhaps I have succeeded in giving expression to this antithesis in a cheerful and affable way — perhaps this writing had no point at all other than to do this. The last thing I would promise would be to 'improve' mankind. I erect no new idols; let the old idols learn what it means to have legs of clay. *To overthrow idols* (my word for 'ideals') — that rather is my business. Reality has been deprived of its value, its meaning, its veracity to the same degree as an ideal world has been *fabricated* ... The 'real world' and the 'apparent world' — in plain terms: the *fabricated* world and reality ... The *lie* of the ideal has hitherto been the curse on reality, through it mankind itself has become mendacious and false down to its deepest instincts — to the point of worshipping the *inverse* values to those which alone could guarantee it prosperity, future, the exalted *right* to a future. (*EH*,33,34)

Following the Foreword, this short passage:

On this perfect day, when everything has become ripe and not only the grapes are growing brown, a ray of sunlight has fallen on my life: I looked behind me, I looked before me, never have I seen so many and such good things together. Not in vain have I buried my forty-fourth year today, I was *entitled* to bury it — what there was of life in it is rescued, is immortal. The first book of the *Revaluation of all Values*, the *Songs of Zarathustra*, the *Twilight of the Idols*, my attempt to philosophize with a hammer — all of them gifts of this year, of its last quarter even! *How should I not be grateful to my whole life?* — And so I tell myself my life. (EH,37)

Nietzsche is not concerned in telling himself of such accomplishments as having become a philosopher, or a philologist, or a physiological psychologist, or a cultural historian, or a poet. Rather, the first Chapter is entitled "Why I Am So Wise." He had become *wise* — that was given priority. And the question of "why," of statement, was asking himself to elaborate on how did this process begin, and how could, or does, he account for being wise? He could have replied to a question such as "How did I become a philosopher, or a philologist?" But instead, becoming wise? Unusual, and obviously in Nietzsche's view, a key issue of concern.

Recall that according to Heraclitus, *wisdom* is best understood as knowing the Logos. And the idea of the Logos is that the world is made up throughout with pairs of opposites, constantly in conflict, but necessarily interdependent. We might add this — that wisdom may be considered as meaning "knowledge of what is true or right, coupled with just judgment as to action, sagacity, discernment, or insight." The opposite of wisdom is stupidity, or ignorance. Heraclitus spoke also of ignorance, suggesting that evil should be understood as meaning "lack of understanding of the Logos." Thomas Hobbes believed that the result of ignorance was calamity.

Evidence that Nietzsche held firmly to Heraclitus' principle of the Logos as the formative principle of the world is everywhere, in all of his writings — what he called his "mask of contrariety." And Nietzsche had become *wise*. Wise may also mean — "having the power, the ability, of discerning and judging properly as to what is true or right; having knowledge or information as to facts, circumstances, etc." The opposite of wise is foolish.

Once more we may be relatively certain of the status of the philosophy of Heraclitus for Nietzsche. It will become clear that these four words from Heraclitus — "Character is man's fate" — served as the formula for Nietzsche's "last testament," of making known to himself who, and what, he had become. Character may mean — "the attributes, distinctive qualities, complex of mental and ethical traits, that distinguish an individual; the aggregate of features and traits that form the individual nature of some person or thing; moral or ethical quality, e.g. honesty or courage." Fate usually implies an inevitable, and often adverse, outcome. Closely related, destiny implies something foreordained, and often suggests a great or noble course, or end.

Section One of the first Chapter of *Ecce Homo*, "Why I Am So Wise," begins with these words:

> The fortunateness of my existence, its uniqueness perhaps, lies in its fatality: to express it in the form of a riddle, as my father I have already died, as my mother I still live and grow old. (*EH*,38)

Consider this. For Nietzsche, *Thus Spoke Zarathustra* had been the telling, or retelling, of his spiritual birth. *Ecce Homo* is the telling, or retelling, of an earlier, natural, physical birth, and of special events and experiences subsequent to that. His very first words speak of his unforeseen, unforetold, good luck, his *fate*. And his "fatality" — the agents, or agency of that fate — are his father and his mother. We need to hear more of what follows:

> This twofold origin, as it were from the highest and the lowest rung of the ladder of life, at once *decadent* and *beginning* — this if anything explains that neutrality, that freedom from party in relation to the total problem of life which perhaps distinguishes me. I have a subtler sense for signs of ascent and decline than any man has ever had, I am the teacher *par excellence* in this matter — I know both, I am both. (*EH*,38)

Nietzsche reminded us earlier that he was a lover of conundrums, puzzles, riddles — drawn to utterance or behavior that is very difficult to interpret; or, to an enigma or problem involving paradox or apparent contradiction; or, to an enigma that challenges ingenuity for its solution. Nietzsche's writing are full of these. And the riddle which begins in these first few lines from *Ecce Homo?*

We are presented with perhaps what was Nietzsche's most important riddle — and this while wearing his "mask of contrariety." In these opening words, he begins with what had been for a long time covered up and uncovered. If you are thinking pairs of opposites, or contraries, the basic, prototypical, eternally recurring opposites in the process of life — natural and cultural — are male and female. In particular, the male as father, and the female as mother. This recognition is rapidly followed by the terms highest and lowest, decadent and beginning, and ascent and decline. These will be followed by many more.

Nietzsche was born in 1844 in the parsonage at Rocken. His father was the village pastor and the son of a pastor. His mother, several years younger (only eighteen years old at Nietzsche's birth), was the daughter of the pastor of a near-by village. Nietzsche was the first child of "this twofold origin," followed by one sister and one brother. His father died when Nietzsche was five.

Nietzsche, I think, in telling his life to himself, sees his father and his mother as having been situated at the time of his birth and early years in a socio-cultural environment which had essentially defined their relationship, actually their "fate." That culture was a Christian culture, which Nietzsche spent much of his active life investigating, exposing, criticizing, and rejecting. Early in his life he understood clearly and emphatically that Christianity had defined a doctrine that placed the male/father on the "highest rung of the ladder of life," and had placed the female/mother on the "lowest rung of the ladder." Nietzsche's family, his "fatality," was his own personal source of being a member of a particular instance of this ladder — what he later calls this "table of values."

His father's destiny had been to become embedded in what Nietzsche, throughout many years, had called this "decadence." His father was "decadent." His mother, the opposite, was "a new beginning." Decadent meaning — "marked by decay or decline." Beginning meaning — "the first part of a process; coming into existence; the point at which something begins." Nietzsche's mother was minutely involved in, or significantly symbolized, some new beginning. He sensed the beginning of the ascent of the female/mother and the decline of the male/father. He *knew* both ascent and decline, he *was* both. This consciousness of his "duality," of this contrariety of his own beginning, played out and defined both his life and his philosophy. We see it at play throughout his writings.

Continuing the passage in Section One, Nietzsche wrote:

> My father died at the age of thirty-six: he was delicate, lovable and morbid, like a being destined to pay this world only a passing visit — a gracious reminder of life rather than life itself. In the same year in which his life declined mine too declined: in the thirty-sixth year of my life I arrived at the lowest point of my vitality — I still lived, but without being able to see three paces in front of me. At that time — it was 1879 — I relinquished my Basel professorship, lived through the summer like a shadow in St. Moritz and the following winter, the most sunless of my life, *as* a shadow in Naumburg. . . Even that filigree art of grasping and comprehending in general, that finger for nuances, that psychology of 'looking around the corner' and whatever else characterizes me was learned only then, is the actual gift of that time in which everything in me became more subtle, observation itself together with all the organs of observation. To look from a morbid perspective towards *healthier* concepts and values, and again conversely to look down from the abundance and certainty of *rich* life into the secret labour of the instinct of *decadence* — that is what I have practised most, it has been my own particular field of experience, in this if in anything I am a master. I now have the skill and knowledge to *invert perspectives*: first reason why a 'revaluation of values' is perhaps possible at all to me alone. — (EH,38,39,40)

That long quotation is almost a distillation of the entire chapter which follows — perhaps of the entire book itself. At least it foreshadows much of what is to come. The dynamics of the process between pairs of opposites continues unabated.

Very often during his writing career, Nietzsche used the many occasions of his spells of severe illness and recovery as opportunities, or experiences, for close observation and reflection. These were experiences of the process, or changes, of opposites available directly. In the above quotation he explains how these frequent episodes influenced his learning something which took on a major significance. Basic to his becoming "wise," he had acquired "the skill and knowledge to invert perspectives." And, he relates this ability to what was rapidly becoming for him his task and his fate — the "revaluation of values."

Little reaching is required to begin to grasp, and to continue in becoming aware, that for Nietzsche, this ability to invert perspectives has as its primary assignment what he had called "the ladder of life." He was able to take a view from the highest down to the lowest, and the reverse. From decadence to beginning, and the reverse. That meant that he had acquired the power to perceive life from the *perspective of the male* and from the *perspective of the female* — to "invert perspectives." This offered the prospect of new interpretations of what he was coming to believe was an unacceptable and destructive structure of the most basic and far-reaching relationship — that between the female and the male — a structure which had been validated and sanctified for centuries.

Earlier Nietzsche had arrived at a radically new way of interpreting perception. All perception, every act of perceiving, is *perspectival*. There is not one single perspective, no "right" perspective, no "wrong" perspective. Rather, there are infinite perspectives — everyone subjective and relative to the perceiving individual. Nietzsche had written earlier:

> . . . today we are at least far from the ridiculous immodesty that would be involved in decreeing from our corner that perspectives are permitted only from this corner. Rather has the world become "infinite" for us all over again, inasmuch as we cannot reject the possibility that *it may include infinite interpretations. (GS,336)*

Nietzsche had been born into a culture-in-process, visible and unmistakable. A culture in transition and transformation — from the old forms which were deteriorating, coming to an end, resisting loudly, violently, the inevitable eventual demise, to the early appearances of new forms, a new beginning. The old forms were being exposed, revealed as a failed experiment (what Nietzsche would claim had been a *lie*). Western culture was vaguely aware of the new form, or forms, struggling to emerge, to replace the old — a developing new experiment.

At an early age Nietzsche had become conscious of being part of the process, and he entered early in actively, vigorously, critically participating. And, very early he had determined that the process was, and would continue being, revolutionary. And, the change was fundamentally a change of *values* — what Nietzsche would frame as a "revaluation of values."

The old forms and values, in a state of stress and growing decay, were the forms and values of religion — of Christianity. But Nietzsche's studies in theology, philosophy, philology, cultural history had persuaded him that this long Christian era had itself emerged centuries earlier, following a long pre-Christian era in which values had been very different. That transformation had also been revolutionary and *negative* in character. It had said "no" to earlier values and forms—easily interpreted as his sense of the dialectic of human cultural history. From a female/mother centered culture to a male/father dominated culture. From a culture that demonstrated and celebrated nature, life, sexuality, procreation, females and males, the body — that said "yes" to one that proclaimed "no." More about this later.

Nietzsche's extended perspectives into the future, his prescience –of this transforming process and of the evolving inevitable conflict which was accompanying it — are shared by the author of *Ecce Homo* later in his book. It is his accumulated wisdom that Nietzsche wants to "give away" in his telling of his own becoming. This wisdom had been woven from his emphases on the conflict of opposites, beginning with, and structured around, the opposites — male and female. It necessarily included and reflected his interest in nature, life, bodies (physiology), powers, ideas, words, values, and much more.

Nietzsche had been born into this changing culture, but at the same moment into the family which was his personal point of entry. Resuming his recounting of his family experiences, from Section Three of "Why I Am So Wise," he wrote:

> This twofold succession of experiences, this accessibility to me of apparently separate worlds, is repeated in my nature if every respect — I am a *Doppelganger*, I have a 'second' face in addition to the first one. (*EH*,41)

And this:

> I regard it as a great privilege to have had such a father: it even seems to me that whatever else of privileges I possess is thereby explained — life, the great Yes to life, *not* included. (*EH*,42)

The privilege of "life, the great Yes to life" was bestowed by his mother, her legacy to him.

Nietzsche occasionally, briefly, played around with his heritage, his genealogy, his lineage, in terms of his nationality and class — his ancestry. Ancestry deals with the line of descent. By the time he wrote *Ecce Homo*, this question of ancestry — with his immediate members, his father and his mother — had become a very different problem. Nietzsche had devoted much of his energy and abilities to revealing the destructive powers of Christianity — especially the values, primarily the moral values. Here in *Ecce Homo* he emphasizes a different perspective, but one which had run through his earlier works. Christianity had come into existence and had developed, endured, and spread with an ideology of "No," while falsely claiming the opposite — what Nietzsche called the "Holy Lie." "No" to this natural world, to life in this world, to the human body, to sexuality (male bodies and female bodies) — and more.

Nietzsche's father was one of the most immediate bearers of this ideology — the messenger and the message. His father was "delicate, lovable and morbid, like a being destined to pay this world only a passing visit — a gracious reminder of life rather than life itself." He died at the age of thirty-six. His morbidity was physiological as well as psychological. Nietzsche's words, "as my father I have already died, as my mother I still live and grow old." Nietzsche had become, not the preacher, but the teacher. He had rejected the pessimism of Christianity (and of atheistic philosophers such as Schopenhauer) and was creating a contrary message — for himself and for others. The process of Western culture had changed, was changing, and would continue to change — a new "Yes" to the old religious "No." And for him, his mother was the living example, his closest ancestor, of this new spirit which had remained dormant for centuries. It was actually a renewal with ancient roots — his Dionysian spirit. Nietzsche had "this two-fold origin."

Perhaps more than anyone else, Nietzsche was out in front in his consciousness of, and understanding of, the Heraclitean revelation of the Logos as the controlling principle of the universe. In ancient Greece, having the religious and philosophical meaning of *wisdom* — divine wisdom. Nietzsche was the philosopher who made his own interpretation of the Logos, of the eternal process of life, rising out of the contraries *female* and *male*, and *affirmation* and *negation*. Was the process of becoming best understood as linear, or logical, or dialectical, or cyclical? I believe Nietzsche incorporated the first three within the fourth — the cyclical. The process was eternally repetitive and was the source of all creativity. This was essentially his wisdom.

There is more in furthering his interpretation. The negative perspectives of Christianity had been directed not only against nature, against life, against the human body, against sexuality and the production of life, but also against the self — against oneself. Deny the self, despise the self, sacrifice the self. One can even see that this was probably the main focus of Nietzsche's moving away from the old degenerate system of values offered by Christianity. What was called for was a complete revaluation of oneself, total affirmation of oneself, responsibility for oneself, respect for oneself, love of oneself. A complete reversal. More of this later. But here in Section Four of "Why I Am So Wise" is this:

> I have never understood the art of arousing enmity towards
> myself — this too I owe to my incomparable father — even
> when it seemed to me very worthwhile to do so. However
> unchristian it may seem, I am not even inimical towards my-

self, one may turn my life this way and that, one will only
rarely, at bottom only once, discover signs that anyone has
borne ill will towards me — perhaps, however, somewhat
too many signs of *good* will . . . My experiences even of those
of whom everyone has bad experiences speak without exception in their favour; I tame every bear, I even make buffoons
mind their manners. During the seven years in which I taught
Greek to the top form of the Basel grammar school I never
once had occasion to mete out a punishment; the laziest were
industrious when they were with me. I am always up to dealing with any chance event; I have to be unprepared if I am to
be master of myself. Let the instrument be what it will, let it
be as out of tune as only the instrument 'man' can become out
of tune — I should have to be ill not to succeed in getting out
of it something listenable. And how often have I heard from
the 'instruments' themselves that they had never heard themselves sound so well. (*EH*,42,43)

Continuing, Section Five reads:

In yet another point I am merely my father once more and
as it were the continuation of his life after an all too early
death. Like anyone who has never lived among his equals
and to whom the concept 'requital' is as inaccessible as is for
instance the concept 'equal rights', I forbid myself in cases
where a little or *very great* act of folly has been perpetrated
against me any counter-measure, any protective measure —
also, as is reasonable, any defence, any 'justification'. My kind
of requital consists in sending after the piece of stupidity as
quickly as possible a piece of sagacity: in that way one may
perhaps overtake it. To speak in a metaphor: I dispatch a pot
of jam to get rid of a *sour* affair . . . Let anyone harm me in any
way, I 'requite' it, you may be sure of that: as soon as I can find
an opportunity of expressing my thanks to the 'offender' (occasionally even for the offence) — or of *asking* him for something, which can be more courteous than giving something.
. . It also seems to me that the rudest word, the rudest let-
ter are more good-natured, more honest than silence. Those
who keep silent almost always lack subtlety and politeness
of the heart; silence is an objection, swallowing down necessarily produces a bad character — it even ruins the stomach.
All those given to silence are dyspeptic. — One will see that
I would not like to see rudeness undervalued, it is the *most
humane* form of contradiction by far and, in the midst of modern tendermindedness, one of our foremost virtues. — If one
is rich enough, it is even fortunate to be in the wrong. A god
come to earth ought to *do* nothing whatever but wrong: to

take upon oneself, not the punishment, but the guilt — only that would be godlike. (*EH*,44,45)

Note above the way — one might say the exaggerated way — in which Nietzsche approaches the characteristic of *honesty*. This quality had continued throughout his development to gain in significance, particularly in contrast to his exploration and disclosure of deception, dishonesty, lies. As he often does with other questions or issues, here he appears to explain and defend honesty in perhaps an unlikely situation. It was that important to him — to become honest and to argue for its place in one's character. He had cautioned that honesty is the "youngest of the virtues." It is fragile and requires nurturing.

If any single element stands out from among the others in Nietzsche's reflecting on his becoming wise, perhaps it is revealed in Section Six. Here are portions of that section:

> Freedom from *ressentiment*, enlightenment over *ressentiment* — who knows the extent to which I ultimately owe thanks to my protracted sickness for this too! The problem is not exactly simple: one has to have experienced it from a state of strength and a state of weakness. If anything whatever has to be admitted against being sick, being weak, it is that in these conditions the actual curative instinct, that is to say the *defensive and offensive instinct* in man becomes soft. One does not know how to get free of anything, one does not know how to have done with anything, one does not know how to thrust back — everything hurts. Men and things come importunately close, events strike too deep, the memory is a festering wound. Being sick *is* itself a kind of *ressentiment*. — . . .

> And nothing burns one up quicker than the affects of *ressentiment*. Vexation, morbid susceptibility, incapacity for revenge, the desire, the thirst for revenge, poison-brewing in any sense — for one who is exhausted this is certainly the most disadvantageous kind of reaction; it causes a rapid expenditure of nervous energy, a morbid accretion of excretions, for example, of gall into the stomach. *Ressentiment* is the forbidden *in itself* for the invalid — *his* evil: unfortunately also his most natural inclination. . .

> *Ressentiment*, born of weakness, to no one more harmful than to the weak man himself — . . .

> He who knows the seriousness with which my philosophy
> has taken up the struggle against the feelings of revengeful-
> ness and vindictiveness even in the theory of "free will" — my
> struggle against Christianity is only a special instance of it
> — will understand why it is precisely here that I throw the
> light on my personal bearing, my *sureness of instinct* in practice.
> (*EH*,45,46)

The central place of ressentiment in Nietzsche's savage critical
interpretation of Christianity was dealt with at some length in my
book, Nietzsche, *Philosopher of the Perilous Perhaps.*

Section Seven of "Why I Am So Wise," adds another aspect of
Nietzsche's reviewing his having become wise:

> War is another thing. I am by nature warlike. To attack is
> among my instincts. *To be able* to be an enemy, to be an en-
> emy — that perhaps presupposes a strong nature, it is in any
> event a condition of every strong nature. It needs resistances,
> consequently it *seeks* resistances: the *aggressive* pathos belongs
> as necessarily to strength as to the feeling of revengefulness
> and vindictiveness does to weakness. Woman, for example,
> is revengeful: that is conditioned by her weakness, just as is
> her susceptibility to others' distress. — The strength of one
> who attacks has in the opposition he needs a kind of *gauge*;
> every growth reveals itself in the seeking out of a powerful
> opponent –or problem: for a philosopher who is warlike also
> challenges problems to a duel. The undertaking is to mas-
> ter, *not* any resistances that happen to present themselves,
> but those against which one has to bring all one's strength,
> suppleness and mastery of weapons — to master *equal* oppo-
> nents. . . Equality in face of the enemy — first presupposition
> of an *honest* duel. Where one despises one *cannot* wage war;
> where one commands, where one sees something as beneath
> one, one *has* not to wage war. — My practice in warfare can
> be reduced to four propositions. Firstly: I attack only causes
> that are victorious — under certain circumstances I wait un-
> til they are victorious. Secondly: I attack only causes against
> which I would find no allies, where I stand alone — where I
> compromise only myself . . . I have never taken a step in pub-
> lic which was not compromising: that is *my* criterion of right
> action. Thirdly: I never attack persons — I only employ the
> person as a strong magnifying glass with which one can make
> visible a general but furtive state of distress which is hard to
> get hold of. . .

Fourthly: I attack only things where any kind of personal difference is excluded, where there is no background of bad experience. On the contrary, to attack is with me a proof of good will, under certain circumstances of gratitude. I do honour, I confer distinction when I associate my name with a cause, a person: for or against — that is in this regard a matter of indifference to me. If I wage war on Christianity I have a right to do so, because I have never experienced anything disagreeable or frustrating from that direction — the most serious Christians have always been well disposed towards me. I myself, an opponent of Christianity *de rigueur*, am far from bearing a grudge against the individual for what is the fatality of millennia. — (EH,47,48)

Anyone would agree, I think, that Nietzsche's "war," and his referring frequently to himself as "warrior," is declaring such a state as meaning the conflict of ideas, or words — never hostile, violent death-dealing war. And this interpretation was expanded in my book, *Nietzsche on War*.

Section Eight of "Why I Am So Wise," begins:

May I venture to indicate one last trait of my nature which creates for me no little difficulty in my relations with others? I possess a perfectly uncanny sensitivity of the instinct for cleanliness, so that I perceive physiologically — *smell* — the proximity or — what am I saying? — the innermost parts, the 'entrails' of every soul . . . I have in this sensitivity psychological antennae with which I touch and take hold of every secret: all the *concealed* dirt at the bottom of many a nature, perhaps conditioned by bad blood but whitewashed by education, is known to me almost on first contact. If I have observed correctly, such natures unendurable to my sense of cleanliness for their part also sense the caution of my disgust: they do not thereby become any sweeter-smelling . . . As has always been customary with me — an extreme cleanliness in relation to me is a presupposition of my existence, I perish under unclean conditions — I swim and bathe and splash continually as it were in water, in any kind of perfectly transparent and glittering element. This makes traffic with people no small test of my patience; my humanity consists, *not* in feeling for and with man, but in *enduring* that I do feel for and with him . . . My humanity is a continual self-overcoming. — But I have need of *solitude*, that is to say recovery, return to myself, the breath of a free light playful air. . . My entire Zarathustra is a dithyramb on solitude or, if I have been understood, on *cleanli-*

ness . . . Disgust at mankind, at the 'rabble', has always been my greatest danger. . . (*EH*,48,49)

We have learned before that Nietzsche possesses "a perfectly uncanny sensitivity" for the "innermost parts" of his own psyche, and it becomes very easy to believe that his sensitivity extended similarly to others. The value of such sensitivity was recognized when he wrote earlier:

Not the strength but the permanence of superior sensibilities is the mark of the superior man. (*BGE*,74)

The disvalue of such sensibilities appears to be that with other people, Nietzsche is aware too often, of too much — speaking psychologically, of course.

Ecce Homo, in its entirety, is Nietzsche's telling to himself the highlights, the details, of the *experiences* of his life — both external and internal. Everything of significance that he perceived, understood, remembered, encountered, participated in, of which he was becoming increasingly conscious, was his material for his amazing story. And Chapter One, "Why I Am So Wise," begins at the beginning of these experiences, and of their recounting.

Fully embracing Heraclitus' interpretation of *wisdom* as "knowledge of the Logos," in this first chapter Nietzsche unequivocally shares with the reader that this had become his guiding principle from the beginning until the end. Chapter One clearly says that Nietzsche's experiences begin with his birth — father and mother, male and female — the prototypical pair of opposites, or contraries, throughout nature. His own individual life process is his personal unique instance of the process of all life. There was a growing awareness for Nietzsche that experiences, although always individual and unique, took two similar but different forms — female and male. These differences in experiences reflected the physiological and psychological differences regarding female and male bodies. The awareness of these differences began early in the development of Nietzsche's thinking and increased dramatically throughout his writing career. The "uncanny dual character" of all living things in nature — *female* and *male*.

Nietzsche has little doubt that every individual, first and foremost, becomes aware of, interested in, concerned with, one's own experiences. And that this characterizes one's entire life process of becoming "what one is." *Who* he was — *this* male child of *this* father and *this* mother. "This twofold succession of experiences, this accessibility to me of apparently separate worlds, is repeated in my nature in every respect — ." One, the father, saying No to life, the other, the mother, saying Yes.

The entire first chapter may be read as Nietzsche's initial recovery of the dynamics of these two additional opposites — Yes and No — in aspects important for "becoming wise." No to enmity, Yes to requiting harm with benefit. A huge No to ressentiment, Yes to becoming warlike in regard to ideas, to causes, with words. And difficulty in saying No, or perhaps Yes, to his disgust in becoming aware of the inner working of many others — given his highly developed sensitivity — his having become a "physiological psychologist."

There are other pairs of opposites in this chapter — decadent and beginning, ascending and descending — but male/father and female/mother, and negative No and affirmative Yes are bedrock. Personally and philosophically.

Before proceeding further into *Ecce Homo*, perhaps this is the proper place to be reminded of how Nietzsche perceived philosophers and philosophy. In the early pages of *Beyond Good and Evil*, written two years prior to *Ecce Homo*, Nietzsche had written this:

> Gradually I have come to realize what every great philosophy up to now has been: the personal confession of its originator, a type of involuntary and unaware memoirs, also that the moral (or amoral) intentions of each philosophy constitute the protoplasm from which each entire plant has grown. Indeed, one will do well (and wisely), if one wishes to explain to himself how on earth the more remote metaphysical assertions of a philosopher ever arose, to ask each time: What sort of morality is this (is *he*) aiming at? Thus I do not believe that a "desire for comprehension" is the father of philosophy, but rather a quite different desire has here as elsewhere used comprehension (together with miscomprehension) as tools to serve its

own ends. Anyone who looks at the basic desires of man with a view to finding out how well they have played their part in precisely this field as inspirational genii (or demons or hob-goblins) will note that they have all philosophized at one time or another. . .

Conversely, there is nothing impersonal whatever in the phi-losopher. And particularly his morality testifies decidedly and decisively as to *who he is* — that is, what order of rank the in-nermost desires of his nature occupy. (*BGE*,6,7)

Nietzsche never deviates from this fundamental interpretation. All philosophizing — serious or superficial — originates and con-tinues to be sustained and grow — from the personal experiences of the philosopher. The personal is philosophical. Or reverse. *Ecce Homo* is an intimate, detailed and I think, honest personal self-por-trait. At the same time, it is Nietzsche's rendering of his philosophical contributions.

PART THREE

Chapter Two of *Ecce Homo*, "Why I Am So Clever," continues as Nietzsche is telling himself his life. (And clever we might think of as meaning — "mentally bright, having sharp or quick intelligence; quick-witted; showing inventiveness or originality; ingenious" — the opposite of stupid or clumsy.) Section One of Chapter Two begins:

> WHY do I know a few *more* things? Why am I so clever altogether? I have never reflected on questions that are none — I have not squandered myself. — I have, for example, no experience of actual *religious* difficulties. I am entirely at a loss to know to what extent I ought to have felt 'sinful'. I likewise lack a reliable criterion of a pang of conscience: from what one *hears* of it, a pang of conscience does not seem to me anything respectable...

> 'God', 'immortality of the soul', 'redemption', 'the Beyond', all of them concepts to which I have given no attention and no time, not even as a child — perhaps I was never childish enough for it? — I have absolutely no knowledge of atheism as an outcome of reasoning, still less as an event: with me it is obvious by instinct. I am too inquisitive, too *questionable*, too high spirited to rest content with a crude answer. God is a crude answer, a piece of indelicacy against us thinkers — fundamentally even a crude *prohibition* to us: you shall not think! I am interested in quite a different way in a question upon which the 'salvation of mankind' depends far more than

it does upon any kind of quaint curiosity of the theologians: the question of *nutriment*. One can for convenience' sake formulate it thus: 'how to nourish yourself so as to attain your maximum of strength, of *virtu* in the Renaissance style, of moraline-free virtue?' — My experiences here are as bad as they possibly could be; I am astonished that I heard this question so late, that I learned 'reason'" from these experiences so late. (EH,51,52)

What follows is a witty account of his experiences with food and drink, but also of his learning and becoming persuaded of the importance of nutriment — individually calculated and regulated for the well-functioning of a person's *body*, and the strength of the body. Nietzsche's very personal experiences of his own body — his many illnesses and recoveries — figured in a major way with the increasing recognition and affirmation of the body and its central importance and role in life. In this passage from Zarathustra, Nietzsche had laid out in a few words just how far his thinking had taken him in this direction:

> I want to speak to the despisers of the body. I would not have them learn and teach differently, but merely say farewell to their own bodies — and thus become silent.
>
> "Body am I, and soul" — thus speaks the child. And why should one not speak like children?
>
> But the awakened and knowing say: body am I entirely, and nothing else; and soul is only a word for something about the body.
>
> The body is a great reason, a plurality with one sense, a war and a peace, a herd and a shepherd. An instrument of your body is also your little reason, my brother, which you call "spirit" — a little instrument and toy of your great reason. (Z,34)

In Section Two, Nietzsche continues in discovering that what makes a difference in one's life are not the "big things" taught by religious education, but rather the "little things." This section begins:

Most closely related to the question of nutriment is the question of *place* and *climate*. No one is free to live everywhere; and he who has great tasks to fulfil which challenge his entire strength has indeed in this matter a very narrow range of choice. The influence of climate on the *metabolism*, its slowing down, its speeding up, extends so far that a blunder in regard to place and climate can not only estrange anyone from his task but withhold it from him altogether: he never catches sight of it. His animalic *vigor* never grows sufficiently great for him to attain to that freedom overflowing into the most spiritual domain where he knows: *that* alone I can do. . .

The *tempo* of the metabolism stands in an exact relationship to the mobility or lameness of the *feet* of the spirit; the 'spirit' itself is indeed only a species of this metabolism. Make a list of the places where there are and have been gifted men, where wit, refinement, malice are a part of happiness, where genius has almost necessarily made its home: they all possess an excellent dry air. Paris, Provence, Florence, Jerusalem, Athens — these names prove something: that genius is *conditioned* by dry air, clear sky — that is to say by rapid metabolism, by the possibility of again and again supplying oneself with great, even tremendous quantities of energy. (*EH*,54,55)

In this section Nietzsche, *from his own experiences*, became further conscious of the results of his life of "ignorance in physiology." He wrote, "I recall with horror the *uncanny* fact that my life up to the last ten years, the years when my life was in danger, was spent nowhere but in the wrong places downright *forbidden* to me." He ends this section with these words:

Any more subtle selfishness, any *protection* by a commanding instinct was lacking, it was an equating of oneself with everyone else, a piece of 'selflessness', a forgetting of one's distance — something I shall never forgive myself. When I was almost done for, *because* I was almost done for, I began to reflect on this fundamental irrationality of my life — 'idealism'. It was only *sickness* that brought me to reason. — (*EH*,56)

It had taken Nietzsche time, and his own experiences of debilitating illness, to become in some sense his own personal physiologist. From neglect, disregard, ignorance, denial of the *body* and its significance, his own body had emerged as demanding and deserving his concern and care — necessary to his energy, and therefore in his view, to his happiness and living well. Yes, an affirmation of *selfishness* as a virtue!

Section Three of "Why I Am So Clever" continues further Nietzsche's reflecting on the process of his having become, not only "wise," but importantly also "clever," and what that means for him:

> Selectivity in nutriment; selectivity in climate and place; — the third thing in which one may at no cost commit a blunder is selectivity in *one's kind of recreation*. Here too the degree to which a spirit is *sui generis* makes ever narrower the bounds of what is permitted, that is to say *useful* to him. In my case all reading is among my recreations: consequently among those things which free me from myself, which allow me to saunter among strange sciences and souls — which I no longer take seriously. It is precisely reading which helps me to recover from my seriousness. At times when I am deeply sunk in work you will see no books around me: I would guard against letting anyone speak or even think in my vicinity. And that is what reading would mean . . . Has it really been noticed that in that state of profound tension to which pregnancy condemns the spirit and fundamentally the entire organism, any chance event, any kind of stimulus from without has too vehement an effect, 'cuts' too deeply? One has to avoid the chance event, the stimulus from without, as much as possible; a kind of self-walling up is among the instinctual sagacities of spiritual pregnancy. Shall I allow a *strange* thought to climb secretly over the wall? — And that is what reading would mean. . . The times of work and fruitfulness are followed by the time of recreation: come hither, you pleasant, you witty, you clever books! . . .
>
> Otherwise I take flight almost always to the same books, really a small number, those books which have *proved* themselves precisely to me. It does not perhaps lie in my nature to read much or many kinds of things: a reading room makes me ill. (EH,56,57)

In this section Nietzsche is further elaborating on his determination to focus attention and *value* on one's self, one's body, one's unique body. The opportunity, the privilege, the developed skill of judicious selecting or choosing, are applicable to these basic bodily desires — and to much more.

In Section Four we learn still more about and from Nietzsche's personal chosen recreations:

> The highest conception of the lyric poet was given me by *Heinrich Heine.* I seek in vain in all the realms of millennia for an equally sweet and passionate music. He possesses that divine malice without which I cannot imagine perfection — I assess the value of people, of races according to how necessarily they are unable to separate the god from the satyr. — And how he employs German! It will one day be said that Heine and I have been by far the first artists of the German language — at an incalculable distance from everything which mere Germans have done with it...
>
> The great poet creates *only* out of his own reality — to the point at which he is afterwards unable to endure his own work... When I have taken a glance at my Zarathustra I walk up and down my room for half an hour unable to master an unendurable spasm of sobbing. — I know of no more heart-rending reading than Shakespeare: what must a man have suffered to need to be a buffoon to this extent! Is Hamlet *understood*? It is not doubt, it is *certainty* which makes mad...But to feel in this way one must be profound, abyss, philosopher... We all *fear* truth... (EH,58,59)

To suggest that Nietzsche loved language, words, the beauty and power of words — including, and especially the words of the poet — is hardly necessary. We have come to realize that with his incomparable insight, Nietzsche had become convinced that the great poet, the creative artist, "one of great imagination and expressive capabilities and special sensitivity to the medium," creates "only out of his own reality." Nietzsche, as Sigmund Freud only vaguely senses, "probably understood more about himself than any man who had ever lived."

Sections Five, Six, and Seven in the chapter "Why I Am So Clever," are Nietzsche's celebrating his gratitude for music as a major recreation in his life and world. A few selected passages may convey the sense and significance of the presence of music for him. Here from Section Five:

> Here where I am speaking of the recreations of my life, I need to say a word to express my gratitude for that which of all things in it has refreshed me by far the most profoundly and

cordially. This was without any doubt my intimate association with Richard Wagner. I offer all my other human relationships cheap; but at no price would I relinquish from my
life the Tribschen days, those days of mutual confidence, of
cheerfulness, of sublime incidents — of *profound* moments. . .
I do not know what others may have experienced with Wagner: over *our* sky no cloud ever passed. — And with that I return again to France — I cannot spare reasons, I can spare a
mere curl of the lip for Wagnerians *et hoc genus omne* who believe they are doing honour to Wagner when they find him
similar to *themselves* . . . Constituted as I am, a stranger in my
deepest instincts to everything German, so that the mere
presence of a German hinders my digestion, my first contact
with Wagner was also the first time in my life I ever drew a
deep breath: I felt, I reverenced him as a being from *outside*,
as the opposite, the incarnate protest against all 'German virtues'.—We who were children in the swamp-air of the fifties
are necessarily pessimists regarding the concept 'German'; we
cannot be anything but revolutionaries — we shall acquiesce
in no state of things in which the *bigot* is on top. It is a matter of complete indifference to me if today he plays in different colours, if he dresses in scarlet and dons the uniform of a
hussar. . . Very well! Wagner was a revolutionary — he fled
from the Germans . . . As an *artist* one has no home in Europe
except in Paris: the *delicatesse* in all five senses of art which
Wagner's art presupposes, the fingers for nuances, the psychological morbidity, is to be found only in Paris. Nowhere
else does there exist such a passion in questions of form, this
seriousness in *mise en scène* — it is the Parisian seriousness *par
excellence*. There is in Germany absolutely no conception of the
tremendous ambition which dwells in the soul of a Parisian
artist. The German is good-natured — Wagner was by no
means good-natured! . . .

What I have never forgiven Wagner? That he *condescended* to
the Germans — that he became *reichsdeutsch* . . . As far as Germany extends it *ruins* culture. — (*EH*,59,60,61)

From Section Six there is more:

All in all I could not have endured my youth without Wagne-
rian music. . . I think I know better than anyone what Wagner
was capable of, the fifty worlds of strange delights to which
no one but he had wings; and as I am strong enough to turn
even the most questionable and most perilous things to my
own advantage and thus to become stronger, I call Wagner
the great benefactor of my life. (*EH*,61)

There was Wagner — every student of Nietzsche knows this. But the place of music in Nietzsche's life goes much beyond that. This from Section Seven:

> I shall say another word for the most select ears: what I really want from music. That it is cheerful and profound, like an afternoon in October. That it is individual, wanton, tender, a little sweet woman of lowness and charm. . . I shall never admit that a German *could* know what music is. What one calls German musicians, the greatest above all, are *foreigners*, Slavs, Croats, Italians, Netherlanders — or Jews: otherwise Germans of the strong race, *extinct* Germans, like Heinrich Schutz, Bach and Handel. I myself am still sufficient of a Pole to exchange the rest of music for Chopin; for three reasons I exclude Wagner's Siegfried Idyll, perhaps also a few things by Liszt, who excels all other musicians in the nobility of his orchestral tone; finally all that has grown up beyond the Alps — *this side* . . . I would not know how to get on without Rossini, even less without *my* south in music, the music of my Venetian *maestro Pietro Gasti*. And when I say beyond the Alps I am really saying only Venice. When I seek another word for music I never find any other word than Venice. I do not know how to distinguish between tears and music — I do not know how to think of happiness, of the *south*, without a shudder of faintheartedness. (*EH*,62)

Section Eight takes Nietzsche further in his discovering, or uncovering, the extent to which his affirmation of oneself had led. He writes:

> In all this — in selection of nutriment, of place and climate, of recreation — there commands an instinct of self-preservation which manifests itself most unambiguously as an instinct for *self-defence*. Not to see many things, not to hear them, not to let them approach one — first piece of ingenuity, first proof that one is no accident but a necessity. The customary word for this self-defensive instinct is *taste*. Its imperative commands, not only to say No when Yes would be a piece of 'selflessness', but also to say No *as little as possible*. To separate oneself, to depart from that to which No would be required again and again. The rationale is that defensive expenditures, be they never so small, become a rule, a habit, lead to an extraordinary and perfectly superfluous impoverishment. Our *largest* expenditures are our most frequent small ones. Warding off, not letting come close, is an expenditure — one should not deceive

oneself over this — a strength *squandered* on negative objectives. One can merely through the constant need to ward off become too weak any longer to defend oneself. —

Another form of sagacity and self-defence consists in *reacting as seldom as possible* and withdrawing from situations and relationships in which one would be condemned as it were to suspend one's 'freedom', one's initiative, and become a mere reagent. (*EH*,63,64)

It is noteworthy here that the issue of the *instincts* is given special attention and particular meaning. The relevance of this affirmation, or reaffirmation, of the instincts becomes increasingly evident if we recall that earlier, especially in both *The Gay Science* and *Beyond Good and Evil*, Nietzsche had unflinchingly insisted on the benefits of recognizing and valuing the instincts, and the dangers involved in any attempt to discredit or ignore them. Here is one typical example:

> *Against the slanderers of nature.* — I find those people disagreeable in whom every natural inclination immediately becomes a sickness, something that disfigures them or is downright infamous: it is *they* that have seduced us to hold that man's inclinations and instincts are evil. *They* are the cause of our great injustice against our nature, against all nature. There are enough people who *might well* entrust themselves to their instincts with grace and without care; but they do not, from fear of this imagined "evil character" of nature. That is why we find so little nobility among men; for it will always be the mark of nobility that one feels no fear of oneself, expects nothing infamous of oneself, flies without scruple where we feel like flying, we freeborn birds. Wherever we may come there will always be freedom and sunlight around us. (*GS*,236)

I suggest these possible meanings of the term "instinct" as close to Nietzsche's understanding and use of this term — "a natural or inherent aptitude or capacity (an instinct for the right word); a largely inheritable and unalterable tendency of an organism to make a complex and specific response to environmental stimuli without involving reason; behavior that is mediated by responses below the conscious level."

In Section Nine Nietzsche unambiguously and definitively makes clear the place he gives to the *self* and to the *instincts* in his own "table of values." And especially, he elaborates on the nuances of the task of "becoming what one is" as this constantly involves these two. He writes:

At this point I can no longer avoid actually answering the question *how one becomes what one is*. And with that I touch on the masterpiece in the art of self-preservation — on *selfish-ness* ... For assuming that the task, the vocation, the *destiny* of the task exceeds the average measure by a significant degree, there would be no greater danger than to catch sight of one-self *with* this task. That one becomes what one is presupposes that one does not have the remotest idea *what* one is. From this point of view even the *blunders* of life — the temporary sidepaths and wrong turnings, the delays, the 'modesties', the seriousness squandered on tasks which lie outside *the* task — have their own meaning and value. They are an expression of a great sagacity, even the supreme sagacity. . . In the mean-time the organizing 'idea' destined to rule grows and grows in the depths — it begins to command, it slowly leads *back* from sidepaths and wrong turnings, it prepares *individual* qualities and abilities which will one day prove themselves indispens-able as means of achieving the whole — it constructs the *an-cillary* capacities one after the other before it gives any hint of the dominating task, of the 'goal', 'objective', 'meaning'. — Regarded from this side my life is simply wonderful. For the task of *revaluation of values* more capacities perhaps were required than have dwelt together in one individual, above all antithetical capacities which however are not allowed to dis-turb or destroy one another. Order of rank among capacities; distance; the art of dividing without making inimical; mixing up nothing, 'reconciling' nothing; a tremendous multiplicity which is nonetheless the opposite of chaos — this has been the precondition, the protracted secret labour and artistic working of my instinct. The magnitude of its *higher protection* was shown in the fact I have at no time had the remotest idea what was growing within me — that all my abilities one day *leapt forth* suddenly ripe, in their final perfection. I cannot re-member ever having taken any trouble — no trace of *struggle* can be discovered in my life, I am the opposite of an heroic na-ture. To 'want' something, to 'strive' after something, to have a 'goal', a 'wish' in view — I know none of this from experi-ence. Even at this moment I look out upon my future — a dis-*tant* future! — as upon a smooth sea: it is ruffled by no desire. I do not want in the slightest that anything should become other than it is; I do not want myself to become other than I am . . . But that is how I have always lived. I have harboured no desire. Someone who after his forty-fourth year can say he has never striven after *honours*, after *women*, after *money!* — Not that I could not have had them . . . Thus, for example, I one day became a university professor — I had never had the remotest thought of such a thing, for I was barely twenty-four years old. Thus two years earlier I was one day a philologist: (*EH*,64,65,66)

What a reversal, a rethinking, a revaluing! This was a major "No" to the dogma of selflessness and the denial of the instincts, and an unprecedented "Yes" in the modern era, to reclaiming, reaffirming, revaluing, praising, trusting the instincts.

It seems appropriate here to remember two particular earlier perspectives of Nietzsche's that pointed ahead in the direction his own instincts, and thinking, were taking him. The first — very early in "Homer's Contest" he wrote:

When one speaks of *humanity*, the idea is fundamental that this is something which separates and distinguishes man from nature. In reality, however, there is no such separation: "natural" qualities and those called truly "human" are inseparably grown together. Man, in his highest and noblest capacities, is wholly nature and embodies its uncanny dual character. Those of his abilities which are terrifying and considered inhuman may even be the fertile soil out of which alone all humanity can grow in impulse, deed, and work. (*PN*,32)

Nietzsche was determined to "renaturalize" humans — to insist on the necessity of re-establishing our "credentials." This is fundamental to trying to continue understanding Nietzsche. Nature, the natural world, is our dwelling place. And instincts are fundamental in our surviving and thriving — as an individual and as a species. Nietzsche was warning that humans must rethink, revalue everything — in order to guarantee the future, our "right to a future."

A second perspective has Nietzsche's attention in this poetical passage from *The Gay Science*, which sounds very much like the "artistic working of my instincts":

One thing is needful.—To "give style" to one's character —a great and rare art! It is practiced by those who survey all the strengths and weaknesses of their nature and then fit them into an artistic plan until every one of them appears as art and reason and even weaknesses delight the eye. Here a large mass of second nature has been added; there a piece of original nature has been removed — both times through long practice and daily work at it. Here the ugly that could not be removed is concealed; there it has been reinterpreted and made sublime. Much that is vague and resisted shaping has been saved and exploited for distant views; it is meant to beckon toward the far and immeasurable. In the end, when the work is finished, it becomes evident how the constraint of a single taste governed and formed everything large and small. Whether this taste was good or bad is less important than one might suppose, if only it was a single taste!. . . For one thing is needful: that a human being should attain satisfaction with himself, whether it be by means of this or that poetry and art; only then is a human being at all tolerable to behold. Whoever is dissatisfied with himself is continually ready for revenge, and we others will be his victims, if only by having to endure his ugly sight. For the sight of what is ugly makes one bad and gloomy. (GS,232,233)

In Section Ten of "Why I Am So Clever," Nietzsche has accumulated a few additional observations of his experiences, which apparently had been working their way during his lifetime, and had become of permanent concern to him. From Section Ten:

I shall be asked why I have really narrated all these little things which according to the traditional judgement are matters of indifference: it will be said that in doing so I harm myself all the more if I am destined to fulfil great tasks. Answer: these little things — nutriment, place, climate, recreation, the whole casuistry of selfishness — are beyond all conception of greater importance than anything that has been considered of importance hitherto. It is precisely here that one has to begin to *learn anew.* Those things which mankind has hitherto pondered seriously are not even realities, merely imaginings, more strictly speaking *lies* from the bad instincts of sick, in the profoundest sense injurious natures — all the concepts 'God', 'soul', 'virtue', 'sin', 'the Beyond', 'truth', 'eternal life'. . .But the greatness of human nature, its 'divinity', has been sought in them. . . All questions of politics, the ordering of society, education have been falsified down to their foundations because the most injurious men have been taken for great men — because contempt has been taught for the 'little' things, which is to say for the fundamental affairs of life. . .Now, when I compare myself with the men who have hitherto been honoured as *pre-eminent* men the distinction is palpable. I do not count these supposed 'pre-eminent men' as belonging to mankind at all — to me they are the refuse of mankind, abortive offspring of sickness and revengeful instincts: they are nothing but pernicious, fundamentally incurable monsters who take revenge on life . . .I want to be the antithesis of this: it is my privilege to possess the highest subtlety for all the signs of healthy instincts. Every morbid trait is lacking in me; even in periods of severe illness I did not become morbid; a trait of fanaticism will be sought in vain in my nature. At no moment of my life can I be shown to have adopted any kind of arrogant or pathetic posture. The pathos of attitudes does *not* belong to greatness; whoever needs attitudes at all is *false* . . . Beware of all picturesque men! Life has been easy for me, easiest when it demanded of me the most difficult things. . . .

I know of no other way of dealing with great tasks than that of *play*: this is, as a sign of greatness, an essential precondition. The slightest constraint, the gloomy mien, any kind of harsh note in the throat are all objections to a man, how much more to his work! . . .

My formula for greatness in a human being is *amor fati*: that one wants nothing to be other than it is, not in the future, not in the past, not in all eternity. Not merely to endure that which happens of necessity, still less to dissemble it — all idealism is untruthfulness in the face of necessity — but to *love* it . . . (EH,66,67,68)

This second chapter, how Nietzsche regards his having become clever, expands and extends his consciousness of his experiences. This entailed a further consideration of particular things which for him were becoming of special interest or concern. And, importantly, a continuation of the necessity of the application of affirmation and negation — of 'yes' or 'no'. His life is emerging as he recognizes and exercises this power, this ability. To be for or against.

Nietzsche says 'no' to non-questions, 'yes' to selected real questions. Then 'no' to selflessness, 'yes' to selfishness. 'No' to big things, 'yes' to little things — to nutriment, place and location, recreation. 'Yes' to things both serious and non-serious, playful. A definite 'yes' to books, to poetry, to music. 'Yes' to the instincts. And a special 'yes' to the instinct which is called "taste" — to the instinct which discerns, judges, appreciates when to say 'no' and when to say 'yes'.

Near the end of this chapter, Nietzsche suggests that these dual, antithetical capacities — the ability to affirm and the ability to negate — are both required for what became his main task, a "revaluation of values." This book, *Ecce Homo*, is his last sketching of that task — his "table of values."

PART FOUR

Chapter Three of *Ecce Homo* is entitled "Why I Write Such Excellent Books." Similar to the first chapter, which was concerned with Nietzsche's becoming wise, and to the second chapter with his becoming clever, the third chapter is concerned with his becoming a writer of excellent books. He *affirms* that he is all of these. And the main threads, or themes, established in the first two chapters remain intact, and easily recognizable.

Section One of Chapter Three, not surprisingly, reiterates, and adds further to, something which had early, and for good reasons, received much of Nietzsche's attention. It is this:

> I AM one thing, my writings are another. — Here, before I speak of these writings themselves, I shall touch on the question of their being understood or *not* understood. I shall do so as perfunctorily as is fitting: for the time for this question has certainly not yet come. My time has not yet come, some are born posthumously. — . . .

> But it would be a complete contradiction of myself if I expected ears *and hands* for *my* truths already today: that I am not heard today, that no one today knows how to take from me, is not only comprehensible; it even seems to me right. I do not want to be taken for what I am not — and that requires that I do not take myself for what I am not. (*EH*,69)

Nietzsche reports on the absurdity and irrelevance of a couple of typical interpretations of his writing. And then continues:

> Through a little trick of chance every sentence here was, with a consistency I had to admire, a truth stood on its head: remarkably enough, all one had to do was to ' revalue all values' in order to hit the nail on the head with regard to me — instead of hitting my head with a nail . . . All the more reason for me to attempt an explanation. –Ultimately, no one can extract from things, books included, more than he already knows. What one has no access to through experience one has no ear for. Now let us imagine an extreme case: that a book speaks of nothing but events which lie outside the possibility of general or even of rare experience — that it is the *first* language for a new range of experiences. In this case simply nothing will be heard, with the acoustical illusion that where nothing is heard there *is* nothing. . . This is in fact my average experience and, if you like, the *originality* of my experience. Whoever believed he had understood something of me had dressed up something out of me after his own image — not uncommonly an antithesis of me, for instance an 'idealist'; whoever had understood nothing of me denied that I came into consideration at all. . .
>
> That I am utterly incurious about discussions of my books, especially by newspapers, will have to be forgiven me. My friends, my publishers know this and do not speak to me about such things. (*EH*,70,71)

Pairs of opposites — understood or not understood, understanding or not understanding. And the time, or times, of his writing was a critical issue. Nietzsche was constantly conscious of the explosive nature of what he was attempting, and of the dangers posed. Earlier he had described himself and his endeavors:

> Every deep thinker fears being understood more than he fears being misunderstood. His vanity may suffer from the latter, but his heart, his fellow-feeling suffers from the former. (*BGE*,230)

And in another place he adds, "You see, I do my best to be understood with difficulty."

Nietzsche earlier had affirmed that the Logos — pairs of contraries — was the overriding theme and principle in all of his thinking and writing. And this is evident throughout. The imaginative, creative expression of this theme, however, would serve as his disguise — as an aid to understanding and at the same time as a deterrent to understanding. He wrote this in *Beyond Good and Evil*:

> Everything deep loves masks; the deepest things have a veritable hatred of image and likeness. Might not *contrariety* be the only proper disguise to clothe the modesty of a god? A question worth asking. It would be surprising if some mystic hadn't at some time ventured upon it. There are events of such delicate nature that one would do well to bury them in gruffness and make them unrecognizable... Such a concealed one, who instinctively uses speech for silence and withholding, and whose excuses for not communicating are inexhaustible, *wants* and encourages a mask of himself to wander about in the hearts and minds of his friends. And if he doesn't want it, one day his eyes will be opened to the fact that the mask is there anyway, and that it is good so. Every thinker needs a mask; even more, around every deep thinker a mask constantly grows, thanks to the continually wrong, i.e. superficial, interpretations of his every word, his every step, his every sign of life. — (BGE46,47)

The insights I find most remarkable in this section are Nietzsche's further references to the significance of the notion of *experience*. "What one has no access to through experience one has no ear for." Experience makes possible more experience, more knowledge, more life. Nietzsche says more than once, "They are unable to hear me."

I think Nietzsche believed that the "excellency" of his books resided in his having written of such ideas, in such a manner or style with words, that these ideas would endure for such a later time as was appropriate and responsive. These books, and the writer of these books, would be heard, found to be exciting, and understood with enthusiasm. Experience was everything.

From serious language about his books, in Section Two Nietzsche reverses to his playful, witty, quizzical distinction between his readers and his non-readers:

This was said for Germans: for I have readers everywhere else — nothing but *choice* intelligences of proved character brought up in high positions and duties; I have even real geniuses among my readers. In Vienna, in St. Petersburg, in Stockholm, in Copenhagen, in Paris and New York — I have been discovered everywhere: I have *not* in Europe's flatland Germany...

A charming Russian lady would not mistake for a moment where I belong. I cannot succeed in becoming solemn, the most I achieve is embarrassment... To think German, to feel German — I can do everything, but *that* is beyond my powers...

We all know, some even know from experience, what a longears is. Very well, I dare to assert that I possess the smallest ears. This is of no little interest to women — it seems to me they feel themselves better understood by me?... (*EH*,71,72)

In Section Three Nietzsche gives exaggerated praise to his writings, but continues identifying his readers:

When I picture a perfect reader, I always picture a monster of courage and curiosity, also something supple, cunning, cautious, a born adventurer and discoverer. Finally: I would not know how to say better to whom at bottom alone I speak than Zarathustra has said it: *to whom* alone does he want to narrate his riddle?

To you, the bold venturers and adventurers, and whoever has embarked with cunning sails upon dreadful seas, to you who are intoxicated with riddles, who take pleasure in twilight, whose soul is lured with flutes to every treacherous abyss — for you do not desire to feel for a rope with cowardly hand; and where you can *guess* to hate to *calculate*... (*EH*,73,74)

Nothing about Nietzsche's writings has been more frequently a subject for criticism, for discrediting his books, than his *style*. In Section Four he replies:

I shall at the same time also say a general word on my *art of style*. To *communicate* a state, an inner tension of pathos through signs, including the tempo of these signs — that is the meaning of every style; and considering that the multiplicity of inner states is in my case extraordinary, there exists in my case the possibility of many styles — altogether the most manifold art of style any man has ever had at his disposal. Every style is *good* which actually communicates an inner state, which makes no mistake as to the signs, the tempo of the signs, the *gestures* — all rules of phrasing are art of gesture. My instinct is here infallible — Good style *in itself* — a piece of pure folly, mere 'idealism', on a par with the 'beautiful *in itself*', the 'good *in itself*', the 'thing *in itself*' . . . Always presupposing there are ears — that there are those capable and worthy of a similar pathos, that those are not lacking to whom one *ought* to communicate oneself. (*EH*,74)

In Nietzsche's view there is no one right style, no "ideal" style. Every style is good which actually communicates an inner state, or a multiplicity of inner states. And the multiplicity of Nietzsche's inner states makes possible many styles. Designed to successfully communicate these inner states, one presupposes there are those who can hear the communication, share the experiences of the writer. In the case of Nietzsche himself, a large measure of these inner states was the awareness of the dangers which characterized his ideas, and his determination to achieve both that he be understood and not understood — at different times. To simultaneously reveal and conceal — and his styles, his adroit use of words, were necessary for his successful legacy.

We may assume that Nietzsche is telling his readers that the contents of his books, from the start, have been this "inner tension of pathos" — this complexity of his *experiences*. And that means of communicating these experiences are intentionally indirect, obscure, disguised, serious, playful, witty, and more. It should not be surprising that Sections Five and Six of "Why I Write Such Excellent Books" reminds us that the person speaking, the person we *may* be able to hear, is a *psychologist*. Earlier he had referred to himself as a 'physiological psychologist'.

In Section Five one gets a sense of urgency, of a rush to say, or say again, some things that must not be left unsaid. This section begins to sound like a crescendo, the hints and buildup of fireworks to follow. These are portions of this section:

That out of my writings there speaks a *psychologist* who has not his equal, that is perhaps the first thing a good reader will notice — a reader such as I deserve, who reads me as good old philologists read their Horace. The propositions over which everybody is in fundamental agreement — not to speak of everybody's philosophers, the moralists and other hollow-heads and cabbage-heads — appear with me as naïve blunders: . . .

The Circe of mankind, morality, has falsified all *psychologica* to its very foundations — has *moralized* it — to the point of the frightful absurdity that love is supposed to be something 'unegoistic' . . . One has to be set firmly upon *oneself*, one has to stand bravely upon one's own two legs, otherwise one *cannot* love at all. In the long run the little women know that all too well: they play the deuce with selfless, with merely objective men . . . Dare I venture in addition to suggest that I *know* these little women? It is part of my dionysian endowment. Who knows? perhaps I am the first psychologist of the eternal-womanly. They all love me — an old story: excepting the *abortive* women, the 'emancipated' who lack the stuff for children. — Happily I am not prepared to be torn to pieces: the complete woman tears to pieces when she loves . . . I know these amiable maenads . . . Ah, what a dangerous, creeping, subterranean little beast of prey it is! And so pleasant with it! . . . A little woman chasing after her revenge would over-run fate itself. — The woman is unspeakably more wicked than the man, also cleverer; goodness in a woman is already a form of *degeneration*. . . At the bottom of all so-called 'beautiful souls' there lies a physiological disadvantage — I shall not say all I could or I should become medicynical. The struggle for *equal* rights is even a symptom of sickness: every physician knows that. — The more a woman is a woman the more she defends herself tooth and nail against rights in general: for the state of nature, the eternal *war* between the sexes puts her in a superior position by far. — have there been ears for my definition of love? It is the only one worthy of a philosopher. Love — in its methods war, in its foundation the mortal hatred of the sexes. Has my answer been heard to the question how one cures — 'redeems' — a woman? One makes a child for her. The woman has need of children, the man is always only the means: thus spoke Zarathustra. (*EH*,75,76)

Just these comments. "The Circe of mankind, morality," would recall the attention in Nietzsche's earlier books to the problem of *morality*. From Homer, Nietzsche very likely was repeating the mythological sense of Circe as "the witch able to transform men into sacrificial swine." And, as I have repeatedly insisted in two earlier books, and will quote again, Nietzsche made clear how he was defining morality. In *Beyond Good and Evil*, this:

> This is why a philosopher should consider himself justified in including willing within the general sphere of morality — morality understood as the doctrine of the rank-relations that produce the phenomenon we call "life." — (*BGE*,21,22)

Morality is doctrine that establishes the ranking between males and females — those who produce "life." And the ranking, in Nietzsche's interpretation, is based on the relative value and power of each of the two sexes. When he refers to himself as an "immoralist," he is asserting his position against such ranking, such a doctrine. He reminded his readers often, (if they needed reminding), that in Western culture, in his era, the inscribed morality was Christian morality — which unequivocally ranked the male above the female, the father above the mother — in power, in value, and in rank. This was also the morality to which he gave the name "slave-morality." Nietzsche has much more to say about morality, or moral values, in later chapters of *Ecce Homo*.

Section Six of the chapter, "Why I Write Such Excellent Books," reads:

> To give an idea of me as a psychologist I take a curious piece of psychology which occurs in 'Beyond Good and Evil' — I forbid, by the way, any conjecture as to whom I am describing in this passage: 'The genius of the heart as it is possessed by that great hidden one, the tempter god and born pied piper of consciences whose voice knows how to descend into the underworld of every soul, who says no word and gives no glance in which there lies no touch of enticement, to whose mastery belongs knowing how to seem — not what he is but what to those who follow him is one constraint *more* to press ever closer to him, to follow him ever more inwardly and thoroughly . . . The genius of the heart who makes everything loud and self-satisfied fall silent and teaches it to listen, who smoothes rough souls and gives them a new desire to savour — the desire to lie still as a mirror, that the deep sky may mirror itself in them . . . The genius of the heart who teaches the stupid and hasty hand to hesitate and grasp more delicately; who divines the hidden and forgotten treasure, the drop of

goodness and sweet spirituality under thick and opaque ice, and is a divining-rod for every grain of gold which has lain long in the prison of much mud and sand . . . The genius of the heart from whose touch everyone goes away richer, not favoured and surprised, not as if blessed and oppressed with the goods of others, but richer in himself, newer to himself than before, broken open, blown upon and sounded out by a thawing wind, more uncertain perhaps, more delicate, more fragile, more broken, but full of hopes that as yet have no names, full of new will and current, full of new ill will and counter current . . .' (*EH*,77)

And the name of the rose? A few scattered subtle hints from Nietzsche suggest that perhaps his "genius of the heart" was "a young charming Russian lady," Fraulein Lou von Salome, or perhaps earlier his young mother "who read to me."

Part Five

Following "Why I Write Such Excellent Books," Nietzsche provides several short chapters, each reflecting briefly on one of his major books. We learn from each one in what ways each has been part of his becoming, as Nietzsche recalls. The following selected passages are offered as further key insights into the messages Nietzsche is communicating, in this narrative of his experiences, of his life. First, his recalling *The Birth of Tragedy*, written in 1872 — with clear and strong indications of where his future thinking would take him:

> Taken up and viewed impartially, the 'Birth of Tragedy' looks very untimely: one would not dream it was begun amid the thunders of the battle of Worth. I thought these problems through before the walls of Metz, in cold September nights while serving in the medical corps; one would rather believe the book to be fifty years older. It is politically indifferent — 'un-German' one would say today — it smells offensively Hegelian, it is in only a few formulas infected with the cadaverous perfume of Schopenhauer. An 'idea' — the antithesis dionysian and apollonian — translated into the metaphysical; history itself as the evolution of this 'idea'; in tragedy this antithesis elevated to a unity; from this perspective things which had never before caught sight of one another suddenly confronted with one another, illuminated by one another and *comprehended*. . . for example opera and revolution . . . The

book's two decisive *novelties* are, firstly the understanding of the *dionysian* phenomenon in the case of the Greeks — it offers the first psychology of this phenomenon, it sees in it the sole root of the whole of Hellenic art — . The other novelty is the understanding of Socratism: Socrates for the first time recognized as an agent of Hellenic disintegration, as a typical *decadent*. 'Rationality' *against* instinct. 'Rationality' at any price as dangerous, as a force undermining life! A profound hostile silence to Christianity throughout the book. It is neither apollonian nor dionysian, it *negates* all *aesthetic* values — the only values the 'Birth of Tragedy' recognizes: it is in the profoundest sense nihilistic, while in the dionysian symbol there is attained the extreme limit of *affirmation*. In one place the Christian priests are alluded to as a 'malicious species of dwarfs', as 'subterraneans' . . .

This beginning is remarkable beyond all measure. I had *discovered* the only likeness and parallel to my own innermost experience which history possesses — I had therewith become the first to comprehend the wonderful phenomenon of the dionysian. By recognizing Socrates as a *decadent* I also offered a quite unambiguous proof of how little the certainty of my psychological grasp stood in danger of influence from any kind of moral idiosyncrasy — morality itself as a symptom of *decadence* is a novelty, a unique event of the first order in the history of knowledge. How high above and far beyond the pitiable shallow-pated chatter about optimism *contra* pessimism I had leapt with these conceptions! — I was the first to see the real antithesis — the *degenerated* instinct which turns against life with subterranean revengefulness (— Christianity, the philosophy of Schopenhauer, in a certain sense already the philosophy of Plato, the whole of idealism as typical forms) and a formula of *supreme affirmation* born out of fullness, of superfluity, an affirmation without reservation even of suffering, even of guilt, even of all that is strange and questionable in existence. . . This ultimate, joyfullest, boundlessly exuberant Yes to life is not only the highest insight, it is also the *profoundest*, the insight most strictly confirmed and maintained by truth and knowledge. . .

— *to realize in oneself* the eternal joy of becoming — the joy which also encompasses *joy in destruction*. . . Before me this transposition of the dionysian into a philosophical pathos did not exist: *tragic wisdom* was lacking — I have sought in vain for signs of it even among the *great* Greeks of philosophy, those of the two centuries *before* Socrates. I retained a doubt in the case of *Heraclitus*, in whose vicinity in general I feel warmer and more well than anywhere else. Affirmation of transitoriness *and destruction*, the decisive element in a dionysian philosophy, affirmation of antithesis and war, *becoming* with a radical rejection even of the concept 'being' — in this I must in any event recognize what is most closely related to me of anything that has been thought hitherto. The doctrine of 'eternal recurrence', that is to say of the unconditional and endlessly repeated circular course of all things — this doctrine of Zarathustra *could* possibly already have been taught by Heraclitus. At least the Stoa, which inherited almost all its fundamental ideas from Heraclitus, shows traces of it. — (*EH*,78,79,80,81)

Nietzsche's early recognition of the Dionysian 'spirit' became a major theme in the remainder of his writings. He often referred to himself as the young god Dionysos, and proclaimed his "dionysian philosophy." As he said, "in the dionysian symbol there is attained the extreme limit of *affirmation*." And Greek Socratism, and especially Christianity which followed, are the antithesis of the dionysian — the extreme limit of *negation*. And he adds:

> A tremendous hope speaks out of this writing. I have in the end no reason whatever to renounce the hope for a dionysian future of music. Let us look a century ahead, let us suppose that my *attentat* on two millennia of anti-nature and the violation of man succeeds. (*EH*,81)

Here Nietzsche is referring to his relentless, devastating critique of Christianity and Christian morality. His final comments on this first book — "the truth about myself spoke out of a dreadful depth."

The Birth of Tragedy (1872) was followed in the next few years by *The Untimely Essays*. And Nietzsche begins his backward glance:

> The four *untimely essays* are altogether warlike. They demonstrate that I was no 'Jack o'Dreams', that I derive pleasure from drawing the sword — also, perhaps, that I have a dangerously supple wrist. The *first* attack (1873) was on German culture, which even at that time I already looked down on with remorseless contempt. Without meaning, without substance, without aim: a mere 'public opinion'. There is no more vicious misunderstanding than to believe that the Germans' great success in arms could demonstrate anything in favour of this culture — not to speak of *its* victory over France. . .

What I am today, *where* I am today — at a height at which I no longer speak with words but with lightning –bolts — oh how far away I was from it in those days! But I *saw* the land — I did not deceive myself as to the way, sea, danger — *and* success! Great repose in promising, this happy looking outward into a future which shall not always remain a promise! — Here every word is experienced, profound, inward; the most painful things are not lacking, there are words in it which are downright bloodsoaked. But a wind of the *great* freedom blows across everything; the wound itself does *not* act as an objection. — How I understand the philosopher, as a fearful explosive material from which everything is in danger, how I remove my concept 'philosopher' miles away from a concept which includes in it even a Kant, not to speak of the academic 'ruminants' and other professors of philosophy: as to this the essay offers an invaluable instruction, even admitting that what is being spoken of is fundamentally not 'Schopenhauer as Educator' but his *opposite*, 'Nietzsche as Educator'. — Considering that my trade was at this time that of a scholar, and perhaps too that I *understood* my trade, an astringent piece of psychology of the scholar which suddenly appears in this essay is not without significance: it expresses *feeling of distance*, my profound certainty as to what can be my *task* and what merely means, interlude and extra. It is my sagacity to have been many things and in many places so as to be able to become *one person* — so as to be able to attain *one thing*. For a time I *had* also to be a scholar. —

I am the first *immoralist* — (EH,84,87,88)

Next followed *Human, All Too Human*, which Nietzsche describes as "progress — towards myself." Reflecting on this book, he writes:

'Human, All Too Human' is the memorial of a crisis. It calls itself a book for *free* spirits: almost every sentence in it is the expression of a victory — with this book I liberated myself from that in my nature which did *not belong to me*. Idealism does not belong to me: the title says: 'where you see ideal things, *I* see — human, alas all too human things!' ... I know humanity better. ... The expression 'free spirit' should here be understood in no other sense: a spirit that has *become free*, that has again seized possession of itself. The tone, the sound of the voice has completely changed: one will find the book sagacious, cool, sometimes harsh and mocking. A certain spirituality of *noble* taste seems to be in constant struggle to keep itself aloft above a more passionate current running underneath. ..

With a torch in hand which gives no trembling light, I illuminate with piercing brightness this *underworld* of the ideal. It is a
war, but a war without powder and smoke, without warlike attitudes, without pathos and contorted limbs — all this would
still have been 'idealism'. One error after another is calmly laid
on ice, the ideal is not refuted — *it freezes* . . . Here for example
'the genius' freezes; on the next corner 'the saint' freezes; 'the
hero' freezes into a thick icicle; at last 'faith', so-called 'convic-
tion', freezes: 'pity' also grows considerably cooler — almost
everywhere 'the thing in itself' freezes. . . (*EH*,89,90)

Human, All Too Human was first published in 1878. In 1886 Nietzsche
also wrote a Preface to this book. He obviously considered these prefaces as elaborations and clarifications of his books. From this Preface
here are a few more words:

Often enough, and always with great consternation, people
have told me that there is something distinctive in all my
writings, from *The Birth of Tragedy* to the most recently published *Prologue to a Philosophy of the Future*. All of them, I have
been told contain snares and nets for careless birds, and an
almost constant, unperceived challenge to reverse one's ha-
bitual estimations and esteemed habits. "What's that? *Everything* is only — human, all too human?" With such a sigh one
comes from my writings, they say, with a kind of wariness
and distrust even toward morality, . . .

Behind his ranging activity (for he is journeying restlessly and
aimlessly, as in a desert) stands the question mark of an ever
more dangerous curiosity. "Cannot *all* values be overturned?".
. .

Here I am, beginning again, doing what I have always done,
the old immoralist and birdcatcher, I am speaking immorally,
extra-morally, "beyond good and evil.". . .

Granted that it is the problem of *hierarchy* which we may call
our problem, we free spirits; only now, in the noonday of our
lives, do we understand what preparations, detours, trials,
temptations, disguises, were needed before the problem *was
permitted* to rise up before us. We understand how we first
had to experience the most numerous and contradictory conditions of misery and happiness in our bodies and souls, as
adventurers and circumnavigators of that inner world which
is called "human being," as surveyors of every "higher" and
"one above the other" which is likewise called "human being,"
penetrating everywhere, almost without fear, scorning noth-

ing, losing nothing, savoring everything, cleaning and virtu-
ally straining off everything of the coincidental — until we
finally could say, we free spirits: "Here is a *new* problem! Here
is a long ladder on whose rungs we ourselves have sat and
climbed, and which we ourselves *were* at one time! Here is a
Higher, a Deeper, a Below-us, an enormous long ordering, a hierarchy which we *see*: here — is *our* problem!" (*HA*,3,4,5,7,10)

Human, All Too Human warrants closer scrutiny. It is recognized as
a seminal book — the beginning of Nietzsche's becoming who and
what he was — personally and philosophically. A process which ter-
minated with *Ecce Homo*. Just these observations. Nietzsche rejects
any notion of some other "real" world — whether that designed by
Plato, by Kant, or by the inventors of the Christian religion. These
other worlds are not accessible and are of no significance to human
beings. There is only this world, this human world. Questions directed toward this other "real" world are empty, non-questions. Questions and problems all develop out of the basic concerns with *what it
means to be human.*

This early book reveals the embryonic stage of Nietzsche's important ideas of will to power and Christian morality. From the beginning, Nietzsche affirms the belief already current that everything has
evolved and is evolving. In this book that meant that we are intro-
duced to the radical idea that truth, or truths, evolve — are relative,
shifting, subjective, never absolute. This was also the case, of course,
with regard to values — always changing, always evolving, always
becoming other. In this book, Nietzsche begins his attack on Christianity and its morality. And he continues his glorification of the pre-
Christian ancient Greek culture and religiosity.

Nietzsche's love of words, his preoccupation and masterful han-
dling of words, are evident throughout this work. Philosophy for him
becomes a task, a narrative addressing that task, with his personal
voice and experiences, his psychology of inner experiences, always in
this and in all later works.

Human, All Too Human starts Nietzsche on his adventure of exploring values — moral values, morality. To shatter old values in order
to make way for new values. We hear a little later his new defini-

tion of *morality*, and as we have said before, have further understanding of his referring to himself as an "immoralist." Failure to imprint this definition on one's psyche would result in failure to understand much of what depends upon this definition and develops from it. This becomes a defining and essential element in his philosophy. In the thinking of a person who held words and speech as a major achievement of being human, and of his awareness of his own ability with words, it would be inconceivable for Nietzsche to have declined in making clear, precise, and unambiguous his definition of morality. And it would be unconscionable for us to ignore his rethinking and redefining. He rejected the conventional meaning of morality as "a doctrine or system of moral conduct, or conformity to ideals of right human conduct." Instead, in *Beyond Good and Evil*, written after *Human, All Too Human*, and before *Ecce Homo*, he made his definition short and unambiguous:

> — morality understood as the doctrine of the rank-relations that produce the phenomenon we call "life." — (*BGE*,22)

An order of rank-relations is a hierarchy, that *new* problem for "free-thinkers." Hierarchy, like a hierarchy of values. Later in *Beyond Good and Evil*, he added this:

> It is obvious that the moral value-characteristics are at first applied to *people* and only later, in a transferred sense, to *acts*. (*BGE*,203)

Make no mistake, *morality* and *moral values*, in Nietzsche's philosophy, are values applied to human beings. And ranking the value of human beings — those who produce the phenomenon we call "life" — male and female — is unconscionable and unacceptable. And much more than that, in Nietzsche's view.

Following *Human, All Too Human*, Nietzsche revisits his book, *Daybreak*. Here are a few passages:

WITH this book begins my campaign against *morality*. Not that it smells in the slightest of gunpowder — quite other and more pleasant odours will be perceived in it, provided one has some subtlety in one's nostrils. . .

The question of the origin of moral values is therefore for me a question of the *first rank* because it conditions the future of mankind. . .

When one directs seriousness away from self-preservation, enhancement of bodily strength, when one makes of green-sickness an ideal, of contempt for the body 'salvation of the soul', what else is it but a *recipe* for *decadence*? — Loss of cen-ter of gravity, resistance to the natural instincts, in a word 'selflessness' — that has hitherto been called *morality*. . . With 'Daybreak' I first took up the struggle against the morality of unselfing. — (*EH*,95,96,97)

After *Daybreak*, which Nietzsche calls an affirmative book, he re-turns his attention to *The Gay Science*. The same applies to this book, he says, "in practically every sentence of this book profundity and exuberance go hand in hand." This book is given only a passing glance in *Ecce Homo*. However, typically, in his Preface written four years af-ter the book itself, there are several additional reflections which are worthy of including in Nietzsche's reviewing for himself just where he is, or was, in his process of becoming who or what he has become. Here are a few reminders from his Preface:

This book may need more than one preface, and in the end there would still remain room for doubt whether anyone who had never lived through similar experiences could be brought closer to the *experience* of this book by means of prefaces. It seems to be written in the language of the wind that thaws ice and snow: high spirits, unrest, contradiction, and April weather are present in it, and one is instantly reminded no less of the proximity of winter than of the triumph over the winter that is coming, must come, and perhaps has already come. . .

This whole book is nothing but a bit of merry-making after long privation and powerlessness, the rejoicing of strength that is returning of a reawakened faith in a tomorrow and the day after tomorrow, of a sudden sense and anticipation of a future, of impending adventures, of seas that are open again, of goals that are permitted again, believed again. . .

For a psychologist there are few questions that are as attractive as that concerning the relation of health and philosophy, and if he should himself become ill, he will bring all of his scientific curiosity into his illness. For assuming that one is a person, one necessarily also has the philosophy that belongs to that person; but there is a big difference. In some it is their deprivations that philosophize; in others, their riches and strengths. The former *need* their philosophy, whether it be as a prop, a sedative, medicine, redemption, elevation, or self-alienation. For the latter it is merely a beautiful luxury — in the best cases, the voluptuousness of a triumphant gratitude that eventually still has to inscribe itself in cosmic letters on the heaven of concepts. . .

The unconscious disguise of physiological needs under the cloaks of the objective, ideal, purely spiritual goes to frightening lengths — and often I have asked myself whether, taking a large view, philosophy has not been merely an interpretation of the body, and a *misunderstanding of the body*.

Behind the highest value judgments that have hitherto guided the history of thought, there are concealed misunderstandings of the physical constitution — of individuals or classes or even whole races. All those bold insanities of metaphysics, especially answers to the question about the *value* of existence, may always be considered first of all as the symptoms of certain bodies. And if such world affirmations or world negations *tout court* lack any grain of significance when measured scientifically, they are the more valuable for the historian and psychologist as hints or symptoms of the body, of its success or failure, its plenitude, power, and autocracy in history, or of its frustrations, weariness, impoverishment, its premonitions of the end, its will to the end.

I am still waiting for a philosophical *physician* in the exceptional sense of that word — one who has to pursue the problem of the total health of a people, time, race or of humanity — to muster the courage to push my suspicion to its limits and to risk the proposition: what was at stake in all philosophizing hitherto was not at all "truth" but something else — let us say, health, future, growth, power, life. . .

We philosophers are not free to divide body from soul as the people do; we are even less free to divide soul from spirit. We are not thinking frogs, nor objectifying and registering mechanisms with their innards removed: constantly, we have to give birth to our thoughts out of our pain and, like mothers, endow them with all we have of blood, heart, fire, pleasure, passion, agony, conscience, fate, and catastrophe. (GS,32,33,34,35,36)

The Prefaces which Nietzsche wrote a few years after each of several of his books are considered small jewels in themselves. As if he discovered more than he had said, than he was aware of having said originally. The Preface to *The Gay Science* is of utmost significance. Waiting for acclamation was the *human body*, the affirmation and celebration of the body. And naturally, Nietzsche's own body. During his relatively brief adult life, he was subject to frequent periods of extreme illness, followed by restored extreme vitality. His body demanded and received his attention and concern. And he was aware of corresponding psychological events — the lows and the highs. *Both* were a necessary aspect of being human. Bodily health and sickness, and psychological health and sickness. And his experiences of debilitating illness and recovery became a model, or metaphor, for cultural debilitation and recovery.

Nietzsche's familiarity with earlier philosophers and their philosophies had led him to interpret them as having been concerned with human bodies by intentionally ignoring , covering up, or misunderstanding the body. And of focusing instead on the soul — especially the "rational" soul — the "invented" soul.

We have yet to hear Nietzsche's story of Zarathustra, or his reminiscences of the experience of writing *Thus Spoke Zarathustra*. However, we may again take note here that the first few lines of the fourth speech of Zarathustra reads as follows:

> I want to speak to the despisers of the body. I would not have them learn and teach differently, but merely say farewell to their own bodies — and thus become silent.

> "Body am I, and soul" — thus speaks the child. And why should one not speak like children?

> But the awakened and knowing say: body am I entirely, and nothing else; and soul is only a word for something about the body. (Z,34)

It was obvious to Nietzsche that his own body was of one form and different from the other *opposite* form. He started his own becoming as a product of his male/father and female/mother. The 'no' sayer, and the 'yes' sayer. The denier and the affirmer. And Nietzsche is unequivocally claiming that oneself, one's own body, is naturally the center of one's own becoming — from start to finish. And he reminded again, that sexuality — male and female — is the prototype of opposites, or contraries.

Following his recollections of *The Gay Science*, Nietzsche attends to what was his next book, *Thus Spoke Zarathustra* — the book which he considered his greatest single gift to humanity. Here are some of his observations that seem to touch the heart of Zarathustra, and thereby of Nietzsche's life and his philosophy:

> I SHALL now tell the story of Zarathustra. The basic conception of the work, the *idea of eternal recurrence*, the highest formula of affirmation that can possibly be attained — belongs to the August of the year 1881: it was jotted down on a piece of paper with the inscription: '6,000 feet beyond man and time'. I was that day walking through the woods beside the lake of Silvaplana; I stopped beside a mighty pyramidal block of stone which reared itself up not far from Surlei. Then this idea came to me.—If I reckon a couple of months back from this day I find as an omen a sudden and profoundly decisive alteration in my taste, above all in music. The whole of Zarathustra might perhaps be reckoned as music; — certainly a rebirth of the art of *hearing* was a precondition of it. In a little mountain resort not far from Vicenza, Recoaro, where I spent the spring of the year 1881, I discovered together with my *maestro* and friend Peter Gast, who was likewise 'reborn', that the phoenix music flew past us with lighter and more luminous wings than it had ever exhibited before. If on the other hand I reckon from that day forwards to the sudden delivery accomplished under the most improbable circumstances in February 1883 — the closing section, from which I have quoted a couple of sentences in the *Foreword*, was completed precisely at that sacred hour when Richard Wagner died in Venice — the pregnancy is seen to have lasted eighteen months. This term of precisely eighteen months might suggest, at least to Buddhists, that I am really a female elephant. (*EH*,99)

> The text, I may state expressly because a misunderstanding exists about it, is not by me: it is the astonishing inspiration of a young Russian lady with whom I was then friendly, Fraulein Lou von Salome. (*EH*,100)

Has anyone at the end of the nineteenth century a distinct conception of what poets of strong ages called *inspiration*? If not, I will describe it. — If one had the slightest residue of superstition left in one, one would hardly be able to set aside the idea that one is merely incarnation, merely mouthpiece, merely medium of overwhelming forces. The concept of revelation, in the sense that something suddenly, with unspeakable certainty and subtlety, becomes *visible*, audible, something that shakes and overturns one to the depths, simply describes the fact. One hears, one does not seek; one takes, one does not ask who gives; a thought flashes up like lightning, with necessity, unfalteringly formed — I have never had any choice. An ecstasy whose tremendous tension sometimes discharges itself in a flood of tears, while one's steps now involuntarily rush along, now involuntarily lag; a complete being outside of oneself with the distinct consciousness of a multitude of subtle shudders and trickles down to one's toes; a depth of happiness in which the most painful and gloomy things appear, not as an antithesis, but as conditioned, demanded, as a *necessary* colour within such a superfluity of light; an instinct for rhythmical relationships which spans forms of wide extent — length, the need for a *wide-spanned* rhythm is almost the measure of the force of inspiration, a kind of compensation for its pressure and tension. . . Everything is in the highest degree involuntary but takes place as in a tempest of a feeling of freedom, of absoluteness, of power, of divinity. . . The involuntary nature of image, of metaphor is the most remarkable thing of all; one no longer has any idea what is image, what metaphor, everything presents itself as the readiest, the truest, the simplest means of expression. It really does seem, to allude to a saying of Zarathustra's, as if the things themselves approached and offered themselves as metaphors (-'here all things come caressingly to your discourse and flatter you: for they want to ride upon your back. Upon every image you here ride to every truth. Here, the words and word-chests of all existence spring open to you; all existence here wants to become words, all becoming here wants to learn speech from you -') This is *my* experience of inspiration; I do not doubt that one has to go back thousands of years to find anyone who could say to me 'it is mine also'.— (*EH*,102,103)

The *body* is inspired: let us leave the 'soul' out of it. . .I could often have been seen dancing; at that time I could walk for seven or eight hours in the mountains without a trace of tiredness. I slept well, I laughed a lot — I was perfectly vigorous and perfectly patient. (*EH*,104)

He contradicts with every word, this most affirmative of all spirits; all opposites are in him bound together into a new unity. (*EH*,106)

But that is the concept of Dionysos himself.—Another consideration leads to the same conclusion. The psychological problem in the type of Zarathustra is how he, who to an unheard of degree says No, *does* No to everything to which one has hitherto said Yes, can nonetheless be the opposite of a spirit of denial; how he, a spirit bearing the heaviest of destinies, a fatality of a task, can nonetheless be the lightest and most opposite — Zarathustra is a dancer — ; how he, who has the harshest, the most fearful insight into reality, who has thought the 'most abysmal thought', nonetheless finds in it no objection to existence, not even to the eternal recurrence of existence — rather one more reason *to be himself* the eternal Yes to all things, 'the tremendous unbounded Yes and Amen' . . . 'Into every abyss I still bear the blessing of my affirmation' . . . *But that is the concept of Dionysos once more.* (*EH*,107,108)

I emphasize one final point: the italicized line provides the occasion. Among the decisive preconditions for a *dionysian* task is the hardness of the hammer, *joy even in destruction*. The imperative 'become hard', the deepest certainty *that all creators are hard*, is the actual mark of a dionysian nature.— (*EH*,111)

The many speeches of Zarathustra are remarkable — often puzzling. The unity of all opposites; the necessary destruction of old values in the process of creating new values; the highest formula of affirmation; and the idea of eternal recurrence. What we are hearing is Nietzsche's "music" — affirmation of the *totality of life*, of the eternal recurrence of life, of the individual who is the "Yes" to life and to himself. Says "Yes" and lives "Yes."

Thus Spoke Zarathustra was soon followed by *Beyond Good and Evil*, subtitled "Prelude to a Philosophy of the Future." And again, Nietzsche reflects back:

THE task for the immediately following years was as clear as it could be. Now that the affirmative part of my task was done, it was the turn of the denying, the No-saying and No-doing part: the revaluation of existing values themselves, the great war — the evocation of a day of decision. Included here is the slow search for those related to me, for such as out of strength would offer me their hand for the *work of destruction*.

— From now on all my writings are fish-hooks: perhaps I understand fishing as well as anyone? . . . If nothing got *caught* I am not to blame. *There were no fish* . . . (*EH*,112)

This book (1886) is in all essentials a *critique of modernity* . . .

Refinement in form, in intention, in the art of *keeping silent*, is in the foreground, psychology is employed with an avowed harshness and cruelty — there is not a single good-natured word in the entire book. (*EH*,112,113)

Nietzsche refers to *Beyond Good and Evil* as a "critique of modernity." It is a book about morality — the morality of the modern age. The morality of the modern age was Christian morality, which in Nietzsche's perspective had been an invention, an error, a failed experiment, a lie — with a long history. And in the first few pages of the book he said plainly how he was defining morality. Again, simply — "the doctrine of rank-relations that produce the phenomenon we call 'life'."

Nietzsche's unrelenting and vicious "campaign against morality" was directed at Christian morality — the ranking of the male/father above the female/mother. A reversal of ranking, a hierarchy of power, of value, of rank was unacceptable. Either order of ranking of the sexes was anathema to Nietzsche — a curse on humanity. And it appears that he did have a historical perspective that envisioned a period of human cultural history in which there was, strictly speaking, no hierarchical relationship. Focus on, or centered on the female/mother — perhaps. This book is Nietzsche's firm, unequivocal, and loudly-voiced "No" to the destructive effects of Christian morality. This in anticipation of a cultural rejection of morality, the "revaluation of existing values themselves, the great war." And, of course, as has been noted, he names himself the "immoralist," as well as the "warrior."

In each succeeding chapter in *Ecce Homo*, Nietzsche has been increasingly removing his "mask of contrariety." And each of his books in succession has been exploring and expanding further these prototypical contraries — female/mother and male/father, and Yes and No. These two pairs of opposites are the basis of morality, or moral values, which in turn are the basis of every culture. His primary interest is Western culture. The old morality had to be demolished to allow for a new beginning, a new paradigm for this relationship.

Nietzsche's Preface to *Beyond Good and Evil* opens with these words:

> Supposing that Truth is a woman — well, now, is there not some foundation for suspecting that all philosophers, insofar as they were dogmatists, have not known how to handle women? That the gruesome earnestness, the left-handed obtrusiveness, with which they have usually approached Truth have been unskilled and unseemly methods for prejudicing a woman (of all people!) in their favor? One thing is certain: she has not been so prejudiced. Today, every sort of dogmatism occupies a dismayed and discouraged position — if, indeed, it has maintained any position at all. (*BGE*,xi)

Nietzsche's *Genealogy of Morals* follows soon after *Beyond Good and Evil*. Of this book he writes:

> The three essays of which this Genealogy consists are in regard to expression, intention and art of surprise perhaps the uncanniest things that have ever been written. Dionysos is, as one knows, also the god of darkness. — Each time a beginning which is *intended* to mislead, cool, scientific, even ironic, intentionally foreground, intentionally keeping in suspense. Gradually an increasing disquiet; isolated flashes of lightning; very unpleasant truths becoming audible as a dull rumbling in the distance — until at last a *tempo feroce* is attained in which everything surges forward with tremendous tension. At the conclusion each time amid perfectly awful detonations a *new* truth visible between thick clouds. — The truth of the *first* essay is the psychology of Christianity: the birth of Christianity out of the spirit of *ressentiment, not*, as is no doubt believed, out of the 'spirit' — essentially a counter-movement, the great revolt against the domination of *noble* values. The *second* essay gives the psychology of the *conscience*: it is *not*, as is no doubt believed, 'the voice of God in man' — it is the instinct of cruelty turned backwards after it can no longer discharge itself outwards. Cruelty here brought to light for the first time as one of the oldest substrata of culture and one that can least be thought away. The *third* essay gives the answer to the question where the tremendous *power* of the ascetic ideal, the priestly ideal, comes from, although it is the *harmful* ideal

par excellence, a will to the end, a *decadence* ideal. Answer: *not* because God is active behind the priests, which is no doubt believed, but *faute de mieux* — because hitherto it has been the only ideal, because it had no competition. 'For man will rather will nothingness than *not* will'. . . What was lacking above all was a *counter-ideal* — *until the advent of Zarathustra.* — I have been understood. Three decisive preliminary studies of a psychologist for a revaluation of all values. — This book contains the first psychology of the priest. (*EH*,114,115)

When Nietzsche says, "Dionysos is, as one knows, also the god of darkness" — remember, he calls himself "Dionysos" and darkness is a symbol of the maternal, the feminine. The dualism of light and dark is a symbolic formula of *morality*. It must be noted here that in *Genealogy of Morals*, Nietzsche has developed the idea of two simultaneous existing orders of moral values — "good vs. bad" and "good vs. evil" — "master-morality" and "slave-morality." Although of these two he prefers "good vs. bad," he is suggesting that we will go beyond both. Contrary to conventional interpretations of these two possible types of morality, I believe they can, and perhaps will, be understood in the future as the two possible ranking orders — female over male and male over female. One active, the other reactive.

In *Beyond Good and Evil*, in addressing the question of the history of morality, Nietzsche had written this:

> — where must our hopes look? We have no other choice: we must seek *new philosophers*, spirits strong or original enough to give an impulse to opposing valuations, to transvalue and turn upside down the "eternal values"; we must seek heralds, men of the future, who will now tie the knot and start the pressure that shall force the will of millenniums to run *new* orbits. (*BGE*,114)

There is much more work to be done, more thinking, more rethinking.

Twilight of the Idols, The Anti-Christ, The Wagner Case, and *Ecce Homo* followed in rapid succession. When Nietzsche takes his backward glance at *Twilight of the Idols* in *Ecce Homo*, he writes this:

THIS writing of fewer than 150 pages, cheerful and fateful in tone, a demon which laughs — the work of so few days I hesitate to reveal their number, is the exception among books: there exists nothing more rich in substance, more independent, more overthrowing — more wicked. If you want to get a quick idea of how everything was upsidedown before me, make a start with this writing. That which is called *idol* on the title page is quite simply that which has hitherto been called truth. *Twilight of the Idols* — in plain terms: the old truth is coming to an end. . . (*EH*,116)

Coming as it does in the later stages of Nietzsche's development, one passage near the end of *Twilight of the Idols* captures the urgency, the passions, the intensity of these last months of his creative life. Here are his words:

I was the first to take seriously, for the understanding of the older, the still rich even overflowing Hellenic instinct, that wonderful phenomenon which bears the name of Dionysus: it is explicable only in terms of an *excess* of force. . . For it is only in the Dionysian mysteries, in the psychology of the Dionysian state, that the *basic fact* of the Hellenic instinct finds expression — its "will to life." What was it that the Hellene guaranteed himself by means of these mysteries? *Eternal* life, the eternal return of life; the future promised and hallowed in the past; the triumphant Yes to life beyond all death and change; *true* life as the over-all continuation of life through procreation, through the mysteries of sexuality. For the Greeks the *sexual* symbol was therefore the venerable symbol par excellence, the real profundity in the whole of ancient piety. Every single element in the act of procreation, of pregnancy, and of birth aroused the highest and most solemn feelings. In the doctrine of the mysteries, *pain* is pronounced holy: the pangs of the woman giving birth hallow all pain; all becoming and growing — all that guarantees a future — involves pain. That there may be the eternal joy of creating, that the will to life may eternally affirm itself, the agony of the woman giving birth *must* also be there eternally.

All this is meant by the word Dionysus: I know of no higher symbolism than this Greek symbolism of the Dionysian festivals. Here the most profound instinct of life, that directed toward the future of life, the eternity of life, is experienced religiously — and the way to life, procreation, as the *holy* way. It was Christianity with its *ressentiment* against life at the bottom of its heart, which first made something unclean of sexuality: it threw *filth* on the origin, on the presupposition of our life. (*PN*,560,561,562)

PART SIX

To the final chapter of *Ecce Homo*, Nietzsche gives the title "Why I Am A Destiny." And it remains the case that his own words tell us more directly what it is that he is communicating. From Section One of this chapter:

> I KNOW my fate. One day there will be associated with my name the recollection of something frightful — of a crisis like no other before on earth, of the profoundest collision of conscience, of a decision evoked *against* everything that until then had been believed in, demanded, sanctified. I am not a man I am dynamite. . .
>
> I was the first to *discover* the truth, in that I was the first to sense — *smell* — the lie as lie. . .My genius is in my nostrils. . . I contradict as has never been contradicted and am nonetheless the opposite of a negative spirit. I am a *bringer of good tidings* such as there has never been, I know tasks from such a height that any conception of them has hitherto been lacking; only after me is it possible to hope again. With all that I am necessarily a man of fatality. But when truth steps into battle with the lie of millennia we shall have convulsions, an earthquake spasm, a transposition of valley and mountain such as has never been dreamed of. The concept politics has then become completely absorbed into a war of spirits, all the power-structures of the old society have been blown into the air — they one and all reposed on the lie: there will be wars

such as there have never yet been on earth. Only after me will there be *grand politics* on earth. — (EH,126,127)

Section Two of this chapter continues:

I am by far the most terrible human being there has ever been; this does not mean I shall not be the most beneficent. I know joy in *destruction* to a degree corresponding to my *strength* for destruction — in both I obey my dionysian nature, which does not know how to separate No-doing from Yes-saying. I am the first *immoralist*: I am therefore the *destroyer par excellence.*— (EH,127)

Moving on to Section Seven, and stressing the same themes as in earlier sections, Nietzsche says this:

Let us here leave the possibility open that it is not mankind which is degenerating but only that parasitic species of man the *priest*, who with the aid of morality has lied himself up to being the determiner of mankind's values — who divines in Christian morality his means to *power*. . .And that is in fact *my* insight: the teachers, the leaders of mankind, theologians included, have also one and all been *decadents: thence* the re-valuation of all values into the inimical to life, *thence* morality . . . *Definition of morality*: morality — the idiosyncrasy of *decadents* with the hidden intention of *revenging themselves on life* — *and* successfully. I set store by *this* definition. — (EH,132,133)

Section Eight, the next to last section of the last chapter of Nietzsche's last book, reads as follows:

Have I been understood?— I have not just now said a word that I could not have said five years ago through the mouth of Zarathustra. — The *unmasking* of Christian morality is an event without equal, a real catastrophe. He who exposes it is a *force majeure*, a destiny — he breaks the history of mankind into two parts. One lives *before* him, one lives *after* him . . . The lightning-bolt of truth struck precisely that which formerly stood highest: he who grasps *what* was then destroyed had better see whether he has anything at all left in his hands. Everything hitherto called 'truth' is recognized as the most harmful, malicious, most subterranean form of the lie; the holy pretext of 'improving' mankind as the cunning to *suck out* life itself and to make it anaemic. Morality as *vampirism*. . . He who unmasks morality has therewith unmasked the valuelessness of all values which are or have been believed in; he no longer sees in the most revered, even *canonized* types of man anything venerable, he sees in them the most fateful kind of abortion, fateful *because they exercise fascination* . . . The concept 'God' invented as the antithetical concept to life — everything harmful, noxious, slanderous, the whole mortal enmity against life brought into one terrible unity! The concept 'the Beyond', 'real world' invented so as to deprive of value the *only* world which exists — so as to leave over no goal, no reason, no task for our earthly reality! The concept 'soul', 'spirit', finally even 'immortal soul', invented so as to despise the body, so as to make it sick — 'holy' — so as to bring to all things in life which deserve serious attention, the questions of nutriment, residence, cleanliness, weather, a horrifying frivolity! Instead of health 'salvation of the soul' — which is to say a *folie circulaire* between spasms of atonement and redemption hysteria! The concept 'sin' invented together with the instrument of torture which goes with it, the concept of 'free will', so as to confuse the instincts, so as to make mistrust of the instincts into second nature! In the concept of the 'selfless', of the 'self-denying' the actual badge of *decadence*, being *lured* by the harmful, no longer being *able* to discover where one's advantage lies, self-destruction, made the sign of value in general, made 'duty', 'holiness', the 'divine' in man! Finally — it is the most fearful — in the concept of the *good* man common cause made with everything weak, sick, ill-constituted, suffering from itself, all that *which ought to perish* — the law of *selection* crossed, an ideal made of opposition to the proud and well-constituted, to the affirmative man, to the man certain of the future and guaranteeing the future — the latter is henceforth called the *evil man*. . .And all this was believed in *as morality*! — *Ecrasez l'infâme*! — (EH,133,134)

Section Nine reads:

— Have I been understood? — *Dionysos against the Crucified* . . . (EH,134)

PART SEVEN

Although there is abundant evidence of the continuing, and I would claim increasing, influence of Nietzsche's wealth of ideas, the radical and revolutionary nature of these ideas remains only partially revealed. The evidence from his writings grows increasingly compelling that we need to consider as the single, simple, profound, overarching, synthesizing, dominating idea — the idea of *change*. That probably most, or all, of his other important ideas radiate from, or revolve around, this idea.

We have seen, or heard, in detail Nietzsche's recording of the changes which he was undergoing in so many different ways. That he was conscious of his experiences as he was becoming different, modified, transformed, converted. Much like the river of Heraclitus, or Nietzsche's own lake or sea, he was the same but not, and never, the same. He gave us a vivid picture of the aspects of his life which seemed especially significant as they were taken up into this continuous changing. His experiences — inner and outer — were brilliantly portrayed. And the process of re-telling was more than that of recording, it was also a process of discovering, or rediscovering.

The extraordinary situation, or perhaps not extraordinary, was that simultaneous with his own individual changing, the culture, the society into which he was born and developing was also visibly changing and evolving. And Nietzsche was clearly aware of, and gravely concerned with, this larger parallel, or larger, process. One needs only to hear his words to sense the excitement, the uncertainty, the tension, the gravity, of the ways in which Nietzsche was perceiving and interpreting the influences, and his responses.

Fully engaged in his own unique personal process of becoming, as he made known to himself in *Ecce Homo*, he was at the same time fully engaged in the cultural changes that were emerging. As he was the principal character in creating himself — what he was becoming — he was also becoming a leading actor in the developing story of his culture. His intentions were those of becoming a major participant in influencing and shaping these changes which were occurring, and would continue to occur. His chosen professional interests provided the credentials and instruments to serve in exceptional ways. To transfer the personal into the philosophical, as well as the reverse. Each of these two adventures provided access, a window, into the other. Or perhaps, each served as a mirror — his personal life reflected his professional life, and his professional life, or philosophical life, reflected his personal life. For him, this dual participation was necessarily the situation. And he was continuously learning from both aspects, both positions, each one informed by the other. His experiences exhibited a kind of reciprocity. He was focusing alternately on himself as an individual, and himself as a participant in the broader contexts — natural and cultural. He viewed himself as necessarily belonging to the world accordingly.

The process of Nietzsche's changing, as he is remembering in detail, from the beginning to near the end, is the story of his life, *Ecce Homo*. During this same time, not only his culture — even more distant and indistinct, his world — was changing. Also his *consciousness* of these experiences and events was correspondingly evolving. He was carefully and conscientiously examining and coming to understand himself, and developing a range of new ideas perhaps unparalleled in history. And most of these ideas, directly or indirectly, are concerned with *change*. If we are to appreciate, understand, and evaluate Nietzsche's legacy, for this and later times, it is our task to focus attention, broadly and deeply, on those ideas which seem to be most significant.

First, a list of issues, or topics, to which Nietzsche as the philosopher directed special attention when considering *change*: names, meanings, definitions, bodies, ideas, beliefs, emotions, desires, aversions, contraries, nature, culture, tastes, opinions, perspectives, interpretations, powers, relations, thoughts, consciousness, truths. Topping his list was the subject, or theme *values* — artistic, religious, ethical, and moral. And from among these — moral values, *morality*.

Nietzsche made little effort to conceal as fundamental his notion that philosophy, or philosophical thinking, required radical changes. New and different ideas, new and different philosophy. What was required was someone to make the form, the content, the future course of philosophy different from what was, had been, or would continue to be if left alone, unchallenged, uncriticized. "Old" philosophy must, and would, be replaced by "new" philosophy. And he assigned the function of defining and effecting these changes primarily to himself.

Here are some of the sweeping changes on Nietzsche's agenda. Philosophy must become: human-centered, humans as belonging to, and participating in, the natural world rather than any supernatural world; scientific, especially physiological and psychological; experimental; historical; reflective of broad expanses of experiences; non-dogmatic; cognizant of the power of speech. And philosophy, or philosophical thinking, must assume as its primary role the creation of *new values*. Changing, or exchanging, old values for new was the primary task looming ahead. And Nietzsche was convinced that this was on the horizon.

Nietzsche's ultimate target, his task, was to become fully armed and fully engaged in efforts to change the *world* — by changing the way we think and feel about the world. The ways we think about, are conscious of, such things as power, power relations, the human body, life, nature, sexuality, values, hierarchies, dualisms or contraries, conflict. And the ways we think about change itself, and feel about change — the possible responses to the reality of the ubiquity of change.

As a 'new psychologist', Nietzsche experienced, and frequently noted, the variety of these responses to change. The range included fear, anger, contempt, hate, envy, disbelief, mistrust, resistance, denial and devaluation of sense experience, avoidance — an array of negative responses. On the contrary, possibilities included acceptance, affirmation, involvement, gratitude. To affirm life, for Nietzsche, implied the necessity of affirming continuous change — everything, eternally, in flux. Change encountered as a threat or as a challenge, an opportunity.

But as with many other ideas, Nietzsche ignored what he might refer to as "change-in-itself," or some abstract notion, or ideal entity, or empty concept or principle. Rather, in the world of human beings — the "human, all too human" world — there were certain prominent activities or aspects, of the process of change, that he selected as demanding his attention. Some of these demand our attention also.

However, a brief pause is helpful to remind of simple, ordinary meanings of the word "change" — "to become, or make different; to make radically different; to give a different position, direction, course; to replace one with another; to shift from one to another."

To better understand Nietzsche's wide-ranging interests and applications, the meanings of a related word "reform" is of additional benefit — "to put or change into an improved form or condition; to amend or improve by change of form or removal of faults or abuses; to put an end to by enforcing or introducing a better method or course of action; to make corrective changes; to make drastic change." As a preview of what is to come, Nietzsche's focus of reform will include *power* structures, orders of *rank*, and tables of *values*.

PART EIGHT

For our century, and for the future beyond, it has become convincingly necessary that we look for new directions, new markers, to help human beings become conscious of where we have been, where we are at present, and how we might have real influence on where we are moving. And I know of no single person more capable of the task than Nietzsche. What follows is my understanding of his roadmap. To say again what are his most outstanding, most valuable (if most volatile) ideas — his *living legacy* to us.

Say that early on Nietzsche asks himself the question — "What does it mean to be human?" Or, "What are the essential aspects of human experience?" His first major investigation in search of answers was perhaps revealed in his book, *Human, All Too Human* in 1878 — a book not welcomed by many of his friends and acquaintances. However, before that book, in 1872, at the early age of twenty-eight, he had written this:

> When one speaks of *humanity*, the idea is fundamental that this is something which separates and distinguishes man from nature. In reality, however, there is no such separation: "natural" qualities and those called truly "human" are insepa-

rably grown together. Man, in his highest and noblest capacities, is wholly nature and embodies its uncanny dual character. (PN,32)

Taking into account that in his late teens, Nietzsche apparently had been recognized as a young scholar in classical studies, and that by 1871 he had applied, if unsuccessfully, for the chair of philosophy at Basel — we may be reasonably certain that he had become fully acquainted with the philosophy of Heraclitus. This pre-Socratic philosopher, Heraclitus — from Nietzsche's earliest philosophical studies; from among all of the other many philosophers with whom he would become familiar; from among those whose thoughts would be important for him — became his favorite and dominated his thinking, determining the course of his personal and philosophical life to the end.

Heraclitus gave to the philosophical community the doctrine of the Logos. In ancient Greek philosophy, the Logos was understood as the controlling principle of the universe. Heraclitus' interpretation of this principle was made clear. His discovery, his recognition, was that the eternal structure of the world is best understood as a unity, consisting entirely of *pairs of opposites*. Neither one of any pair is capable of existing on its own. Opposites are interdependent and constantly in a stage of change in relation one to the other — what Heraclitus called "conflict". This principle applies whether one is considering the natural world or the socio-cultural world. It appears that Heraclitus, as did Nietzsche, believed that humans are generally ignorant of the Logos and remain essentially so, even when they hear it explained. One principle, denoting or serving to make known, the fundamental nature of all reality — *dualism*, or *dualisms*. Heraclitus' "truth" and Nietzsche's "truth".

In *Ecce Homo*, when Nietzsche is reminiscing about the memorable experience of the inspiration and writing of his enigmatic, cryptic, mysterious *Thus Spoke Zarathustra*, he says this regarding Zarathustra:

> The ladder upon which he climbs up and down is tremendous; he has seen further, willed further, *been able* further than any other human being, He contradicts with every word, this

most affirmative of all spirits; all opposites are in him bound together into a new unity. The highest and the lowest forces of human nature, the sweetest, most frivolous and most fearsome stream forth out of *one* fountain with immortal certainty. Until then one does not know what height, what depth is; one knows even less what truth is. There is no moment in this revelation of truth which would have been anticipated or divined by even *one* of the greatest. There is no wisdom, no psychology, no art of speech before Zarathustra: the nearest things, the most everyday things here speak of things unheard of. (*EH*,106)

The title of Nietzsche's book which followed soon after *Thus Spoke Zarathustra* shouts loudly and clearly the call to listen. This book was *Beyond Good and Evil*, to which he gave the subtitle "Prelude to a Philosophy of the Future". In *Ecce Homo* Nietzsche refers back to *Beyond Good and Evil* and says this:

The task for the immediately following years was as clear as it could be. Now that the affirmative part of my task was done, it was the turn of the denying, the No-saying and *No-doing* part: the revaluation of existing values themselves, the great war — the evocation of a day of decision. Included here is the slow search for those related to me, for such as out of strength would offer me their hand for the *work of destruction*. — From now on all my writings are fish-hooks: perhaps I understand fishing as well as anyone?. . . If nothing got *caught* I am not to blame. *There were no fish*. . . (*EH*,112)

In the early pages of *Beyond Good and Evil* Nietzsche had written:

Everything deep loves masks; the deepest things have a veritable hatred of image and likeness. Might not *contrariety* be the only proper disguise to clothe the modesty of a god? A question worth asking. It would be surprising if some mystic hadn't at some time ventured upon it. There are events of such delicate nature that one would do well to bury them in gruffness and make them unrecognizable. . . Such a concealed one, who instinctively uses speech for silence and withholding, and whose excuses for not communicating are inexhaustible, *wants* and encourages a mask of himself to wander about in the hearts and minds of his friends. And if he doesn't want it, one day his eyes will be opened to the fact that the mask is there anyway, and that it is good so. Every deep thinker needs a mask; even more around every deep thinker a mask constantly grows, thanks to the continually wrong, i.e. superficial, interpretation of his every word, his every step, his every sign of life. — (BGE,46,47)

Opposites, contraries, uncanny dualisms — an informing principle, a dominating theme, in all of Nietzsche's thinking and writing. And as with Heraclitus — wisdom is affirming and understanding the Logos. Ignorance, or failure in understanding, was to court catastrophe. No other philosopher comes close to Nietzsche in exploring and expanding, in affirming and celebrating, this interpretation of reality.

From Nietzsche's love of words, his delight and expertise in the playfulness and possibilities of words, and his awareness of the power of words, it follows that a great deal of his writing seems obscure, difficult, mysterious, puzzling. He affirmed his attraction to puzzles, conundrums, riddles, puns, metaphors, and more. And Zarathustra was his first major accomplishment at puzzling, or riddling. *Ecce Homo* was his final riddle — a riddle for which the solution was embedded within the riddle itself. This last book was the story of his life *and* it served also as his final making clear to himself and to certain of his readers, his philosophy — what he had discovered as the special and essential elements, or aspects, of "being human".

So, we will revisit *Ecce Homo*, giving even closer attention to Nietzsche's final unsystematic system — his philosophical reflecting on the Logos, personal and philosophical. We will try, perhaps clumsily, to join him in ruminating on those "uncanny dualisms". These are the opening words of the Foreword of *Ecce Homo*:

> SEEING that I must shortly approach mankind with the heaviest demand that has ever been made on it, it seems to me indispensable to say *who I am*. (EH,33)

Soon following are the opening words of the first chapter, "Why I Am So Wise":

> THE fortunateness of my existence, its uniqueness perhaps, lies in its fatality: to express it in the form of a riddle, as my father I have already died, as my mother I still live and grow old. (*EH*,38)

Nietzsche, with no hesitation, with no equivocation, with no effort at concealment, is affirming and re-affirming what is the *prototype of all opposites*. The instance of dualism upon which all efforts to answer the questions directed at the possible meaning of "being human" depend, and from which they radiate, is the dualism of father/mother, male/female. The God of Christianity knew this, and Noah had it right. And as a young scholar in Basel, with the Swiss mythologist and cultural historian, J. J. Bachofen, as his mentor, Nietzsche added exponentially to his supporting evidence — if any was needed. Every additional aspect of this focus on dualisms which follows throughout the book to the last climax — to morality and immorality — is a development or further elaboration on the fundamental, eternal, inescapable pair of opposites — female and male.

The phenomenon we call "life" is produced, is created, by this interdependent pair. All life — but of most interest, human life, the continuous process of life — is an expression, with finer distinctions, of this dualism. Philosophy, if concerned with humanity, as it claims to be and should be, must build on this fundamental fact. This is precisely what Nietzsche does. Never forget, or doubt however, that he is creating his philosophy in the form of a *riddle*.

Continuing his recounting, Nietzsche wrote:

> This twofold origin, as it were from the highest and the lowest rung of the ladder of life, at once *decadent* and *beginning* — this if anything explains that neutrality, that freedom from party in relation to the total problem of life which perhaps distinguishes me. I have a subtler sense for signs of ascent and decline than any man has ever had, I am the teacher *par excellence* in this matter — I know both, I am both. (*EH*,38)

In this small segment of the opening paragraph we have these opposites — dead and alive, highest and lowest, decadent and beginning, ascent and decline. All of these are being used to interpret, from Nietzsche's perspectives, the cultural situation into which he was cast. His fate was, or would become, his response to momentous changes in German culture — changes involving two directions, two places, two conditions. And he will elaborate further. The term "decadent" reappears frequently and gains in importance. Decadent, or decadence — meaning "presupposes reaching and passing the peak of development and implies a turn downward with a consequent loss of vitality or energy, e.g. cultural decadence." It suggests a loss of value, or decay.

Nietzsche's father, the village pastor and son of a pastor, serves as the symbol, or face, of the decadence, of the declining power of the Christian religion. The line of descent which he represents, of which he is a participant, of which he was an advocate and a messenger, was in decline. And this was one part of Nietzsche's own genealogy. At the same time, his mother serves as a symbol, or face, of the beginning of a young opposing power. And this was the other part of Nietzsche's inheritance, his fate. Of himself, he said, "Setting aside the fact that I am a *decadent*, I am also its antithesis." As the son of his father, Nietzsche's "fatality" was descending. As the son of his mother, the opposite was the case. His "fatality" was ascending — in the beginning stages of reversing.

Nietzsche made his own experience, his clear consciousness of this experience, the subject or source of his reflecting — of his philosophy. That is what a philosopher is, or does. Especially acute, and demanding attention, were Nietzsche's frequent episodes of severe illness, weakness, and pain — physiological. These periods were followed by periods of physical exuberance, strength, energy, creativity. As a major natural physiological recurrence, this part of his experience served as a model for many applications in addressing psychological and cultural issues or problems. These experiences, closely examined, offered for Nietzsche a wide range of possibilities for interpreting psychological and cultural processes, or change. From focus on the individual body to attention to situations and events, experience other than the body. But never doubt, in Nietzsche's life and in his philosophy, the human body — one's own body — remains the defining concern, and it is always in a process of change. The ground of all essential elements, or aspects, of being human is this — *you are this body*. And in Nietzsche's thinking, one's responses to one's own body — affirmation or denial, love or hate, care or neglect, etc., take first place in terms of priorities. To his listeners, Nietzsche's Zarathustra proclaimed, "to despisers of the body, let them die." And the psyche is always *about* the body — so we are told. The prototype of all opposites — male and female — may be additionally expressed as two bodies — male body and female body. Nietzsche's father and his mother — the sexual human bodies, the essential element of being human.

In *Ecce Homo*, after recounting with clarity the immediacy of his becoming ill and that of becoming healthy, Nietzsche wrote:

> After all this do I need to say that in questions of *decadence* I am *experienced*? I have spelled it out forwards and backwards. Even that filigree art of grasping and comprehending in general, that finger for nuances, that psychology of 'looking around the corner' and whatever else characterizes me was learned only then, is the actual gift of that time in which everything in me became more subtle, observation itself together with all the organs of observation. To look from a morbid perspective toward *healthier* concepts and values, and again conversely to look down from the abundance and certainty of *rich* life into the secret labour of the instinct of *decadence* — that is what I have practiced most, it has been my own particular field of experience, in this if in anything I am a master. I now have the skill and knowledge to *invert perspectives*: first reason why a 'revaluation of values' is perhaps possible at all to me alone.— (*EH*,39,40)

This passage is rich in its ability, in relatively few words, to connect several of these dualisms. We should note that in the opening paragraph Nietzsche had written these words also:

> My father died at the age of thirty-six: he was delicate, lovable and morbid, like a being destined to pay this world only a passing visit — a gracious reminder of life rather than life itself. (*EH*,38)

Turning his attention to the element of perception is a further major step. In earlier writing Nietzsche had developed persuasively the idea that all perception is a matter of *perspective*, and that there are an infinite number of perspectives, along with an infinite number of interpretations of these perspectives. We perceive an infinite number of 'things' — self, others, bodies, words, images, energy, power, dualisms, change — to name a few. All perceiving is perspectival — perspectives which are constantly changing. Perceiving is a primary aspect of human experience, of what it means to be human. Now Nietzsche has further refined and extended this notion, and will continue to do this. He has affirmed that he is able to "invert perspectives".

Nietzsche had discovered the dualistic possibilities of perspectives. "I looked behind me, I looked before me." Now he adds, he is able to look "from a morbid perspective towards *healthier* concepts and values—to look up. And "conversely to look down from the abundance and certainty of *rich* life . . ." He was able to reproduce for himself the perspectives of his "delicate, lovable, and morbid father." But, he is now able to "invert perspectives" — to look at life from the perspectives of his mother. He is able to see different ideas, and most importantly, different values, to consider new possibilities for a necessary "revaluation of values".

One would not discredit Nietzsche in saying that he appears to become increasingly convinced that *everything* that we can know, or feel, has its source in *experience*. The concept, or word, experience reveals the richness of what is being thought through. Experience may mean "direct observation of, or participation in, events as a basis of knowledge; the fact or state of having been affected by or gained knowledge through direct observation or participation; practical knowledge, skill, or practice derived from direct observation or participation in events or in a particular activity; the conscious events that make up an individual life; the events that make up the conscious past of a community or nation or mankind generally; something personally encountered, undergone, or lived through; the act or process of directly perceiving events or reality."

After Nietzsche refers to his having become a master of "my own particular field of experience," and has acquired the skill and knowledge to "invert perspectives," he continues:

> This twofold succession of experiences, this accessibility to me of apparently separate worlds, is repeated in my nature in every respect — I am a *Doppelganger*, I have a 'second' face in addition to the first one. *And* perhaps also a third . . . Even by virtue of my descent I am permitted to look beyond all merely locally, merely nationally conditioned perspectives, it costs me no effort to be a 'good European'. (*EH*, 11)

The significance of Nietzsche's consciousness of there being two distinct modes of experiences — one male, the other female, cannot be over emphasized when interpreting and understanding Nietzsche's philosophy. It would no longer be possible to philosophize on the basis of the unexamined claim that all human experiences are variations of some single basic type. "Two apparently separate worlds" — but each accessible to the other. This proclamation would have unforeseen implications and possibilities. The notion "lived experience" never has a meaning which is either monolithic or abstract. The substructure of all life is that there are *two* very different modes of experience.

It should be noted here that the reporting by Nietzsche that having the skill and knowledge which allows one to "invert perspectives" has implications for other situations. It is repeatable and applicable in the context of nationality, or race, or class, or religion. For him, this skill and knowledge has become part of his "nature". No longer what Heidegger later referred to as "one-sided view and one-track thinking." There is much more to be heard on this pair of opposites — this dualism.

After briefly tracing his ancestry — factual or fictional — Nietzsche says:

> I regard it as a great privilege to have had such a father: it even seems to me that whatever else of privileges I possess is thereby explained — life, the great Yes to life, *not* included. Above all that it requires no intention on my part, but only

a mere waiting, for me to enter involuntarily into a world of exalted and delicate things: I am at home there, my innermost passion becomes free only there. That I paid for this privilege almost with my life is certainly no unfair trade. — To understand anything at all of my Zarathustra one has perhaps to possess a qualification similar to that which I possess — to have one foot *beyond* life . . . (EH,42)

These few words, perhaps more than any single passage in the book, ask for elaboration. Familiarity with much of Nietzsche's earlier writing is necessarily assumed in his summary of the essential opposites that infused his thinking, which centered on what being human really means.

Nietzsche was not a logician. The recognition of the notion of affirmation and denial in formal thought was of little concern to him, and he developed his own critique of logic. However, the significance of this dualism, of saying "yes" and saying "no", reflect the "most primitive acts of thought." Nietzsche's recognition, interpretation, and application of these fundamental thoughts/words — "yes" and "no" — are amazing and alarming. And they remain in the mainstream of his thinking. It could be suggested that together with the pair, male and female, the pair of affirmation and negation, probably form the very ground of Nietzsche's philosophy.

Nietzsche's relentless and ruthless critique of Christianity had probed deeply into what he perceived as the sources of its continuing cruelty and its devastatingly destructive power in Western culture. The core of this religion, he revealed, was the abominable and ridiculous ranking system which valued and ranked the male/father over the female/mother. Centuries of writing and rewriting, of updating the message and methods of enforcement, had resulted in privileging the male and unprivileging the female. (The focus of my recent book, *Nietzsche, Philosopher of the Perilous Perhaps*, is a detailed account of his critique.)

In Nietzsche's interpretation of Christianity, while he often dealt with the obvious issue of sexuality surreptitiously, he screamed and thundered, that Christianity from the beginning had voiced a loud "no" to nature, to life, to the human body, to sexuality, and particularly to the female and the female body. No passage captures more immediately the resonance of Nietzsche's thinking than these words at the end of *Twilight of the Idols*:

> I was the first to take seriously, for the understanding of the older, the still rich even overflowing Hellenic instinct, that wonderful phenomenon which bears the name of Dionysus: it is explicable only in terms of an *excess* of force . . . For it is only in the Dionysian mysteries, in the psychology of the Dionysian state, that the *basic fact* of the Hellenic instinct finds expression — its "will to life." What was it that the Hellene guaranteed himself by means of these mysteries? *Eternal* life, the eternal return of life; the future promised and hallowed in the past; the triumphant Yes to life beyond all death and change; *true* life as the over-all continuation of life through procreation, through the mysteries of sexuality. For the Greeks the *sexual* symbol was therefore the venerable symbol par excellence, the real profundity in the whole of ancient piety. Every single element in the act of procreation, of pregnancy, and of birth aroused the highest and most solemn feelings. In the doctrine of the mysteries, *pain* is pronounced holy: the pangs of the woman giving birth hallow all pain; all becoming and growing — all that guarantees a future — involves pain. That there may be the eternal joy of creating, that the will to life may eternally affirm itself, the agony of the woman giving birth *must* also be there eternally.
>
> All this is meant by the word Dionysus: I know of no higher symbolism than this Greek symbolism of the Dionysian festivals. Here the most profound instinct of life, that directed toward the future of life, the eternity of life, is experienced religiously — and the way to life, procreation, as the *holy* way. It was Christianity, with its *ressentiment* against life at the bottom of its heart, which first made something unclean of sexuality: it threw *filth* on the origin, on the presupposition of our life. (PN,560,561,562)

Nietzsche's pastor father, "delicate, lovable, and morbid" though he may have been, was a messenger, delivering the message Nietzsche came to revile. His father shared in what Nietzsche believed was a decadent, decaying, descending, dying view of life. And Nietzsche was, in an unavoidable way, his father's son. It was part of his "fatality". The privileges which he has been granted, the entitlements which had accrued to him in being male, were those received from his father.

The opposing view — "the great Yes to life" — which he has taken as his own, and would have others acclaim as well, was the "privilege" which he owed to his mother. Nietzsche was becoming increasingly aware of the intimations of a beginning, an emerging, ascending response to nature, life, the body, sexuality. And of the prospect of a revaluation of values, in which he was taking part. He was his mother's son — part of his "fatality".

Nietzsche's often-questioned "eternal recurrence" may be interpreted as a return of the Dionysian mysteries, the total affirmation of, and celebration of, life. But saying "yes" to *life* means saying "yes" to many other "yeses" and "noes".

To his "incomparable father" Nietzsche attributes two models — psychological or behavioral — which have become notable in marking him as "merely my father once more and as it were the continuation of his life after an all too early death." Nietzsche ventures that he has never understood, never experienced, enmity toward either himself or others. Also, he has learned well to requite harm from another with some token benefit. His interpretation here mentions the issue of honesty, but this will be dealt with later.

Unique in Nietzsche's philosophical development is the use that he makes of one dominant aspect of his own personal experience — the dialectic between sickness and recovery. This continuing contrast, his consciousness of the alternating changes, his careful reflection on each state, becomes a source of many of his unusual ideas — physiological, and especially psychological. These experiences also gave rise to further rethinking of the process of revaluation — to which he had committed himself. We have already seen how Nietzsche uses the importance of the condition of *decadence*. The decadent, sick, declining-in-health, individual and the decadent, decaying, deteriorating culture are mirror situations. Perhaps the two are closely correlated.

In *Ecce Homo*, Nietzsche again uses the dialectic of sickness and health to advance his thinking on an emotion, or passion, i.e. a subjective response to a person or situation, partly mental and partly physical. This psychological phenomenon was *ressentiment*. The importance of ressentiment cannot be overstated, particularly in his radically new and dangerous interpretation of the psychological source of Christianity and the decadence of the Christian view of life. In this lengthy passage he again revisits the issue:

> Freedom from *ressentiment*, enlightenment over *ressentiment* —
> who knows the extent to which I ultimately owe thanks to
> my protracted sickness for this too! The problem is not ex-
> actly simple: one has to have experienced it from a state of
> strength and a state of weakness. If anything whatever has
> to be admitted against being sick, being weak, it is that in
> these conditions the actual curative instinct, that is, to say the
> *defensive and offensive instinct* in man becomes soft. One does not
> know how to get free of anything, one does not know how to
> have done with anything, one does not know how to thrust
> back — everything hurts. Men and things come importu-
> nately close, events strike too deep, the memory is a festering
> wound. Being sick *is* itself a kind of *ressentiment*. — Against
> this the invalid has only one great means of cure — I call it
> *Russian fatalism*, that fatalism without rebellion with which a
> Russian soldier for whom the campaign has become too much
> at last lies down in the snow. No longer to take anything at
> all, to receive anything, to take anything *into* oneself — no
> longer to react at all . . . The great rationality of this fatalism,
> which is not always the courage to die but can be life-preser-
> vative under conditions highly dangerous to life, is reduction
> of the metabolism, making it slow down, a kind of will to hi-
> bernation. A couple of steps further in this logic and one has
> the fakir who sleeps for weeks on end in a grave . . . Because
> one would use oneself up too quickly *if* one reacted at all, one
> no longer reacts: this is the logic. And nothings burns one
> up quicker than the affects of *ressentiment*. Vexation, morbid
> susceptibility, incapacity for revenge, the desire, the thirst
> for revenge, poison-brewing in any sense — for one who is
> exhausted this is certainly the most disadvantageous kind of
> reaction: it causes a rapid expenditure of nervous energy, a
> morbid accretion of excretions, for example of gall into the
> stomach. *Ressentiment* is the forbidden *in itself* for the invalid
> — his evil: unfortunately also his most natural inclination. —
> This was grasped by that profound physiologist Buddha. His
> 'religion', which one would do better to call a *system of hygiene*
> so as not to mix it up with such pitiable things as Christian-
> ity, makes its effect dependant on victory over *ressentiment*: to
> free the soul of *that* — first step to recovery. 'Not by enmity is
> enmity ended, by friendship is enmity ended': this stands at
> the beginning of Buddha's teaching — it is not *morality* that
> speaks thus, it is physiology that speaks thus. — *Ressentiment*,
> born of weakness, to no one more harmful than to the weak
> man himself — in the opposite case, where a rich nature is the

presupposition, a *superfluous* feeling to stay master of which is almost the proof of richness. He who knows the seriousness with which my philosophy has taken up the struggle against the feelings of revengefulness and vindictiveness even into the theory of 'free will' — my struggle against Christianity is only a special instance of it — will understand why it is precisely here that I throw the light on my personal bearing, my *sureness of instinct* in practice. In periods of *decadence* I *forbade* them to myself as harmful; as soon as life was again sufficiently rich and proud for them I forbade them to myself as *beneath* me. That 'Russian fatalism' of which I spoke came forward in my case in the form of clinging tenaciously for years on end to almost intolerable situations, places, residences, company, once chance had placed me in them — it was better than changing them, than *feeling* them as capable of being changed — than rebelling against them ... In those days I took it deadly amiss if I was disturbed in this fatalism, if I was forcibly awakened from it — and to do this was in fact every time a deadly dangerous thing. — To accept oneself as a fate, not to desire oneself 'different' — in such conditions this is *great rationality* itself. (*EH*,45,46,47)

In the dialectic of affirmation and denial, of 'yes' and 'no', the latter becomes a drumbeat when Nietzsche is considering ressentiment, which is usually accompanied by revenge, or the desire for revenge. A resounding 'no' to Christianity and to the ressentiment from which it originates, and to revenge. Wisdom, in Nietzsche's thinking, requires as a major element, the elimination of the poison of ressentiment and revenge. R. J. Hollingdale, in his book *Nietzsche*, reflecting on Nietzsche as the psychologist of will to power, wrote this:

What is desired, according to this theory, is the feeling of increased power. The negative aspect, that is to say the feeling of impotence, of being subject to the power of another, produces as its characteristic effect the phenomenon of *ressentiment* — and this is the chief corollary of the theory of will to power. Nietzsche developed the psychology of resentment almost as luxuriently as he did that of power: the essence of it is that the powerless man feels resentment against those whose power he feels and against this state of powerlessness itself and out of this feeling of resentment *takes revenge* — on other people or on life itself. The objective of the revenge is to get rid of the feeling of powerlessness; the forms it takes include all moralities in which punishment is a prominent feature; all doctrines of future damnation (of the powerful) and salvation (of the powerless); the socialist millennium, with the class at present oppressed on top and the present ruling class exterminated or in labour camps; anarchism, which Nietzsche saw as a peculiarly direct and uncomplicated expression of the resentment of impotence; in short, every kind of open or disguised revenge. (N,183,184)

And what about war, struggle, conflict, competition between opposing forces? Nietzsche writes:

War is another thing. I am by nature warlike. To attack is among my instincts. *To be able* to be an enemy, to be an enemy — that perhaps presupposes a strong nature, it is in any event a condition of every strong nature. It needs resistances, consequently it *seeks* resistances: the *aggressive* pathos belongs as necessarily to strength as the feeling of revengefulness and vindictiveness does to weakness. (*EH*,47)

Nietzsche's "warlike nature" expresses itself in the conflict of ideas. He challenges problems, resistant problems, to which he must bring all of his "strengths, suppleness, and mastery of weapons" — his words. This is the "best of all possible wars." As for hostile, violent, armed conflict — like Christianity, it is "anti-life", a major ingredient of decadence.

Clearly Nietzsche has begun his thinking about human experience with his natural base. There are males and females. There are male bodies and female bodies, male experiences and female experiences — "two worlds". Nietzsche then turns his attention to two other distinctions when thinking about experiences. *Outer experience* — simply put, the engagement with other bodies in motion, in space, physiological, and all other external phenomena. And particularly the experiences involving human bodies. And more particularly, female bodies and male bodies.

Then there is *inner experience* — all internal phenomena, which in Nietzsche's interpretation, always correlates or corresponds with external experience. As a "physiological psychologist", his concerns were directed more toward psychology as an emerging new science which promised unforeseen, unexplored possibilities for understanding the human world. He had been recording important aspects of his consciousness of his own inner experiences. And then he changes, inverts his perspectives, to include how he perceives the internal phenomena of others. He writes this:

> May I venture to indicate one last trait of my nature which creates for me no little difficulty in my relations with others? I possess a perfectly uncanny sensitivity of the instinct for cleanliness, so that I perceive physiologically — *smell* — the proximity or — what am I saying? — the innermost parts, the 'entrails', of every soul . . . I have in this sensitivity psychological antennae with which I touch and take hold of every secret: all the *concealed* dirt at the bottom of many a nature, perhaps conditioned by bad blood but whitewashed by education, is known to me almost on first contact. If I have observed correctly, such natures unendurable to my sense of cleanliness for their part also sense the caution of my disgust: they do not thereby become any sweeter-smelling . . . As has always been customary with me — an extreme cleanliness in relation to me is a presupposition of my existence, I perish under unclean conditions — I swim and bathe and splash continually as it were in water, in any kind of perfectly transparent and glittering elements. This makes traffic with people no small test of my patience; my humanity consists, not in feeling for and with man, but in *enduring* that I do feel for and with him . . . My humanity is a continual self-overcoming. — But I have need of *solitude*, that is to say recovery, return to myself, the breath of a free light playful air. . . My entire Zarathustra is a dithyramb on solitude or, if I have been understood, on *cleanliness*. . .Fortunately not on *pure folly*. — He who has eyes for colours will call it diamond. — *Disgust* at mankind, at the 'rabble', has always been my greatest danger. . . (EH,48,49)

Nietzsche had spent so much of himself in describing what he perceived as a destructive culture, deteriorating conditions, and had assigned the primary responsibility for this, of course, to Christianity and its morality. His perspectives on others, those whom he refers to as the "rabble"; his disgust at the "innermost parts" of every psyche; his awareness that he shares with others those features which are the sources of disgust — these experiences he sees as his greatest danger. Escape from disgust, redemption from disgust — as was freedom from ressentiment — was necessarily a step in becoming "wise".

Wisdom, in Nietzsche's personal life, and in his philosophy, was wisdom "Heraclitean-style". It was understanding and affirming those "uncanny dualisms". It meant understanding the basics of being human — of being either male or female — plus the basics of either affirming or denying. Yes to life, yes to honesty, yes to war. No to enmity, no to ressentiment, no to disgust. From much of what Nietzsche had written prior to *Ecce Homo*, the reader may plausibly infer that everything that has been said thus far is referring to the duality of the sexes. This wisdom requires remorsefully learning from experience — past and present.

PART NINE

In speaking of dualisms, there is more. In the chapter, "Why I Am
So Clever," Nietzsche begins:

> WHY do I know a few *more* things? Why am I so clever alto-
> gether? I have never reflected on questions that are none — I
> have not squandered myself. — I have, for example, no expe-
> rience of actual *religious* difficulties. I am entirely at a loss to
> know to what extent I ought to have felt 'sinful'. I likewise
> lack a reliable criterion of a pang of conscience: from what one
> *hears* of it, a pang of conscience does not seem to me anything
> respectable . . . I should not like to leave an act in the lurch
> *afterwards*, I would as a matter of principle prefer to leave the
> evil outcome, the *consequences*, out of the question of values.
> When the outcome is evil one can easily lose the *true* eye for
> what one has done: a pang of conscience seems to me a kind of
> '*evil* eye'. To honour to oneself something that went wrong all
> the more *because* it went wrong — that rather would accord
> with my morality. — 'God', 'immortality of the soul', 'redemp-
> tion', 'the Beyond', all of them concepts to which I have given
> no attention and no time, not even as a child — perhaps I was
> never childish enough for it? — I have absolutely no knowl-
> edge of atheism as an outcome of reasoning, still less as an
> event: with me it is obvious by instinct. I am too inquisitive,
> too *questionable*, too high spirited to rest content with a crude
> answer. God is a crude answer, a piece of indelicacy against
> us thinkers — fundamentally even a crude *prohibition* to us:
> you shall not think! . . . I am interested in quite a different way

in a question upon which the 'salvation of mankind' depends far more than it does upon any kind of quaint curiosity of the theologian: the question of *nutriment*. One can for convenience' sake formulate it thus: 'how to nourish yourself so as to attain your maximum of strength, of *virtu* in the Renaissance style, of moraline-free virtue?' My experiences here are as bad as they possibly could be; I am astonished that I heard this question so late, that I learned 'reason' from these experiences so late. (*EH*,51,52)

This distinction between questions and non-questions is followed by a delightful, spirited discussion of German cookery, French diet, and English diet. Also, wine, tea, alcohol, water, big meals versus small meals, the size of one's stomach, sitting versus walking. What is important is that attention be paid, on a very individual basis, to one's digestion, one's stomach. A healthy diet, good nutriment, is a necessary condition for the energy, the feeling of power, the well-functioning of the body. What else? The body is *who* you are. These are some of the *real* questions, not those posed, for example, by the "quaint curiosity of the theologian". These things he learned, some early, some late.

Nietzsche is saying that the opposition is not between questions which can be answered and those which you are unable to answer. Rather, the latter are non-questions, for the notion of a question itself is that its opposite is an answer. Nietzsche continues:

Most closely related to the question of nutriment is the question of *place* and *climate*. No one is free to live everywhere; and he who has great tasks to fulfil which challenge his entire strength has indeed in this matter a very narrow range of choice. The influence of climate on the *metabolism*, its slowing down, its speeding up, extends so far that a blunder in regard to place and climate can not only estrange anyone from his task but withhold it from him altogether: he never catches sight of it. His animalic *vigor* never grows sufficiently great for him to attain to that freedom overflowing into the most spiritual domain where he knows: *that* I alone can do . . . A never so infinitesimal sluggishness of the intestines grown into a bad habit completely suffices to transform a genius into something mediocre, something 'German'; the German climate alone is enough to discourage strong and even heroic intestines. The *tempo* of the metabolism stands in an exact relation-

ship to the mobility or lameness of the *feet* of the spirit; the
'spirit' itself is indeed only a species of this metabolism. Make
a list of the places where there are and have been gifted men,
where wit, refinement, malice are a part of happiness, where
genius has almost necessarily made its home: they all possess
excellent dry air. Paris, Provence, Florence, Jerusalem, Athens
— these names prove something: that genius is *conditioned* by
dry air, clear sky — that is to say by rapid metabolism, by the
possibility of again and again supplying oneself with great,
even tremendous quantities of energy. (*EH*,54,55)

Nietzsche reflects further, expressing consternation and alarm at
his ignorance in physiology, his education in "accursed idealism" —
ideas far removed from what was needed for life. Physiology trumps
theology. He writes:

When I was almost done for, *because* I was almost done for, I
began to reflect on this fundamental irrationality of my life
— 'idealism'. It was only *sickness* that brought me to reason.
— (*EH*,56)

Continuing his surprising interpretation, concentrating still on
what being human really means, Nietzsche writes:

Selectivity in nutriment; selectivity in climate and place; —
the third thing in which one may at no cost commit a blunder
is selectivity in *one's kind of recreation*. Here too the degree to
which a spirit is *sui generis* makes ever narrower the bounds of
what is permitted, that is to say *useful* to him. In my case all
reading is among my recreations: consequently among those
things which free me from myself, which allow me to saun-
ter among strange sciences and souls — which I no longer
take seriously. It is precisely reading which helps me to re-
cover from *my* seriousness. At times when I am deeply sunk in
work you will see no books around me: I would guard against
letting anyone speak or even think in my vicinity. And that
is what reading would mean . . . Has it really been noticed
that in that state of profound tension to which pregnancy
condemns the spirit and fundamentally the entire organism,
any chance event, any kind of stimulus from without has too
vehement an effect, 'cuts' too deeply? One has to avoid the
chance event, the stimulus from without, as much as possible;
a kind of self-walling-up is among the instinctual sagacities

> of spiritual pregnancy. Shall I allow a *strange* thought to climb
> secretly over the wall? — And that is what reading would
> mean . . . The times of work and fruitfulness are followed by
> the time of recreation: come hither, you pleasant, you witty,
> you clever books! (*EH*,56)

Each important pair of contraries receives separate attention. Recognizing the constant connectedness of pairs, nevertheless any single pair admits of, and needs, elaboration of the place, and function, and value, of each one of the pair. The contrast and special status of both work and non-work, work and play, work and recreation, has been a theme throughout Nietzsche's writing. Almost to say that play comes first, followed by work, followed by the realization of the value of *both* — the necessity and reality of both. Like waking and sleeping. Marx had given his skills to interpreting work. Nietzsche at times sounds as if he is interpreting and preferring play or recreation — the Dionysian festivals, or the child. For Nietzsche, both work and recreation — for him writing and reading — are indispensable to life. For any person, the duality of the serious and the non-serious is a major aspect, among countless others, of what it means to be human. Having accepted the Logos — the fundamental nature of contraries — this idea, or principle, becomes Nietzsche's basic key of interpreting human existence. All of nature is an exhibition of these contraries, or dualisms, and humans as part of nature exhibit exactly this pattern, and participate in this order.

We know Nietzsche's short life was crowded with his 'serious' work, the books he wrote. But along with these, complementing and enriching this part, were the books he read. Beyond the books, he finds much satisfaction in retelling to himself his love of poetry — and especially the lyric poetry of Heinrich Heine. And he reflects deeply on his love of music, necessarily recounting his experience as a youth in responding to the music of Richard Wagner. Nietzsche's acquaintances, friends, and disciples know that his original 'yes' in response to Wagner later became a 'no'.

Nietzsche ends his contemplation on the music in his life with these words:

> I shall say another word for the most select ears: what I really want from music. That it is cheerful and profound, like an afternoon in October. That it is individual, wanton, tender, a little sweet woman of lowness and charm... (*EH*,62)

Nietzsche explores deeply and extensively the fundamental ubiquity and the ambiguity of the dualism 'yes' and 'no' when one becomes conscious of its presence and importance for life — and for *who* you are and what you become. He continues:

> In all this — in selection of nutriment, of place and climate, of recreation — there commands an instinct of self-preservation which manifests itself most unambiguously as an instinct for *self-defence*. Not to see many things, not to hear them, not to let them approach one — first piece of ingenuity, first proof that one is no accident but a necessity. The customary word for this self-defensive instinct is *taste*. Its imperative commands, not only to say No when Yes would be a piece of 'selflessness', but also to say *No as little as possible*. To separate oneself, to depart from that to which No would be required again and again. The rationale is that defensive expenditures, be they never so small, become a rule, a habit, lead to an extraordinary and perfectly superfluous impoverishment. Our *largest* expenditures are often our most frequent small ones. Warding off, not letting come close, is an expenditure — one should not deceive oneself over this — a strength squandered on negative objectives. One can merely through the constant need to ward off become too weak any longer to defend oneself...
>
> Another form of sagacity and self-defence consists in *reacting as seldom as possible* and withdrawing from situations and relationships in which one would be condemned as it were to suspend one's 'freedom', one's initiative, and become a mere reagent. (*EH*,63,64)

This nuanced discussion of affirmation and denial is another instance of the subtlety of the relationship of 'yes' and 'no' to strength and weakness, to the expenditure or preservation of energy — physical and psychological. This brief discussion also leads to another of these basic dualisms and revaluations. Nietzsche had repeatedly deplored and spoken against the belief in, or practice of, selflessness, particularly as advocated, if not demanded, by the Christian religion. Here he adds to his revaluation in support of its opposite:

> At this point I can no longer avoid actually answering the question *how one becomes what one is*. And with that I touch on the masterpiece in the art of self-preservation — of *selfishness* . . .

> That one becomes what one is presupposes that one does not have the remotest idea *what* one is. From this point of view even the *blunders* of life — the temporary sidepaths and wrong turnings, the delays, the 'modesties', the seriousness squandered on tasks which lie outside *the* task — have their own meaning and value. They are an expression of a great sagacity, even the supreme sagacity: . . .

> In the meantime the organizing 'idea' destined to rule grows and grows in the depths — it begins to command, it slowly leads *back* from the sidepaths and wrong turnings, it prepares *individual* qualities and abilities which will one day prove themselves indispensable as means to achieving the whole — it constructs the *ancillary* capacities one after the other before it gives any hint of the dominating task, of the 'goal', 'objective', 'meaning'. — Regarded from this side my life is simply wonderful. For the task of a *revaluation of values* more capacities perhaps were required than have dwelt together in one individual, above all antithetical capacities which however are not allowed to disturb or destroy one another. Order of rank among capacities; distance; the art of dividing without making inimical; mixing up nothing, 'reconciling' nothing; a tremendous multiplicity which is nonetheless the opposite of chaos — this has been the precondition, the protracted secret labour and artistic working of my instincts. . .

> Thus, for example, I one day became a university professor — I had never had the remotest thought of such a thing, for I was barely twenty-four years old. Thus two years earlier I was one day a philologist: . . (*EH*,64,65,66)

One of the 'sacrifices' which Nietzsche claims Christianity has required of the individual is the sacrifice, or denial, of the instincts in favor of some plan or goal. He is reclaiming the legitimacy, the importance, the power of the instincts in humans as an organizing principle of the process of "becoming what one is." And he would suggest that the capacities, the powers, of any individual will unfold if confidence is restored in the functioning of these instincts — the instincts of affirmation and negation. It is clear that Nietzsche became passionately engaged in restoring the instincts, the imagination, the intuition, the emotions, to their valuable place in the overall pattern of human experience.

Just this note. The notion, or word "instinct" usually means — "a natural or inherent aptitude, impulse, or capacity; a largely inheritable and unalterable tendency of an organism to make a complex and specific response to environmental stimuli without involving reason." The responses of 'yes' or 'no', it appears, may be deliberative or they may be instinctive, and in Nietzsche's view the value of the latter is probably greater.

Finishing this part of his story of his having become clever, having attained a different and additional kind of knowledge, Nietzsche writes:

> I shall be asked why I have really narrated all these little things which according to the traditional judgement are matters of indifference: it will be said that in doing so I harm myself all the more if I am destined to fulfil great tasks. Answer: these little things — nutriment, place, climate, recreation, the whole casuistry of selfishness — are beyond all conception of greater importance than anything that has been considered of importance hitherto. It is precisely here that one has to begin to *learn anew.* Those things which mankind has hitherto pondered seriously are not even realities, merely imaginings, more strictly speaking *lies* from the bad instincts of sick, in the profoundest sense injurious natures — all the concepts 'God', 'soul', 'virtue', 'sin', 'the Beyond', 'truth', 'eternal life' . . . But the greatness of human nature, its 'divinity', has been sought in them. . . All questions of politics, the ordering of society, education have been falsified down to their foundations because the most injurious men have been taken for great men — because contempt has been taught for the 'little' things, which is to say for the fundamental affairs of life. . . (*EH*,66,67)

PART TEN

Nietzsche certainly has given new meaning to the idea of *wisdom*, taking Heraclitus as his mentor. He has adopted the principle of dualism, pairs of opposites, in unprecedented ways. He has "accumulated philosophical or scientific learning." He has great and deep understanding of human beings and situations — of *human experience*. He believes, affirms, and demonstrates that, and how, he has become wise, and that he desires to give to others this wisdom. Remember Zarathustra.

Also, he has developed his own interpretation of the idea of *cleverness* from his own experience. He has the special aptitude, or power, of inventing, or discovering, or originating, often with wit and ingenuity. He has become clever. Wisdom and cleverness — apparently what Nietzsche considers as two of his most valuable attributes, or qualities. And he reveals them in detail to himself and to his readers. Which brings him to reflect further.

The next chapter of *Ecce Homo* is entitled "Why I Write Such Excellent Books." The short, simple answer — in order to share, to make known, this wisdom and this cleverness. He begins:

I am one thing, my writings are another. — Here, before I speak of these writings themselves, I shall touch on the question of their being understood or *not* understood. I shall do so as perfunctorily as is fitting: for the time for this question has certainly not yet come. My time has not yet come, some are born posthumously. — One day or other institutions will be needed in which people live and teach as I understand living and teaching: perhaps even chairs for the interpretation of Zarathustra will be established. But it would be a complete contradiction of myself if I expected ears *and hands* for *my* truths already today: that I am not heard today, that no one today knows how to take from me, is not only comprehensible; it even seems to me right. I do not want to be taken for what I am not — and that requires that I do not take myself for what I am not. (*EH*,69)

Nietzsche suggests that to have understood his Zarathustra, one would have had to *experience* parts of the book. But understanding and misunderstanding, being understood and not being understood, is a major theme of his. Earlier he had written:

Every deep thinker fears being understood more than he fears being misunderstood. His vanity may suffer from the latter, but his heart, his fellow-feeling suffers from the former. (*BGE*.230)

In "Why I Write Such Excellent Books," he continues:

Ultimately, no one can extract from things, books included, more than he already knows. What one has no access to through experience one has no ear for. Now let us imagine an extreme case: that a book speaks of nothing but events which lie outside the possibility of general or even of rare experience — that it is the *first* language for a new range of experiences. In this case simply nothing will be heard, with the acoustical illusion that where nothing is heard there *is* nothing . . . This is in fact my average experience and, if you like, the *originality* of my experience. Whoever believed he had understood something of me had dressed up something out of me after his own image — not uncommonly an antithesis of me, for instance an 'idealist'; whoever had understood nothing of me denied that I came into consideration at all. . . (*EH*,70,71)

These are a few more of Nietzsche's perspectives on his readers and his non-readers:

> That I am utterly incurious about discussions of my books, especially by newspapers, will have to be forgiven me. My friends, my publishers know this and do not speak to me about such things. . .

> This was said for Germans: for I have readers everywhere else — nothing but *choice* intelligences of proved character brought up in high positions and duties; I have even real geniuses among my readers. In Vienna, in St. Petersburg, in Stockholm, in Copenhagen, in Paris and New York — I have been discovered everywhere: I have *not* been in Europe's flat-land Germany . . . And to confess it, I rejoice even more over my non-readers, such as have never heard either my name or the word philosophy; but wherever I go, here in Turin for example, every face grows more cheerful and benevolent at the sight of me. What has flattered me the most is that old market-women take great pains to select together for me the sweetest of their grapes. This is *how far* one must be a philosopher. . .

> A charming Russian lady would not mistake for a moment where I belong. I cannot succeed in becoming solemn, the most I can achieve is embarrassment. . . To think German, to feel German — I can do everything but *that* is beyond my powers. . .

> We all know, some even know from experience, what a longears is. Very well, I dare to assert that I possess the smallest ears. This is of no little interest to women — it seems to me they feel themselves better understood by me?...I am the *anti-ass par excellence* and therewith a world-historical monster — I am, in Greek and not only in Greek, the *Anti-Christ*. . . (EH,71,72)

Nietzsche describes his books, as he sees them, and also imagines the wide variety of responses which perhaps have been, or might be, evoked in reading his books. He finally says this:

> When I picture a perfect reader, I always picture a monster of courage and curiosity, also something supple, cunning, cautious, a born adventurer and discoverer. Finally: I would not know how to say better to whom at bottom alone I speak

than Zarathustra has said it: *to whom* alone does he want to narrate his riddle?

To you, the bold venturers and adventurers, and whoever has embarked with cunning sales upon dreadful seas,

to you who are intoxicated with riddles, who take pleasure in twilight, whose soul is lured with flutes to every treacherous abyss –

for you do not desire to feel for a rope with cowardly hand; and where you can *guess* to hate to *calculate*. . . (EH,73,74)

Nietzsche's *Ecce Homo* is his summary of how he had become a philosopher — wise, clever, a thinker, a writer of books — a lover of wisdom. And what these books revealed — what his philosophy was, or had become. Also, to whom he was speaking that philosophy, what his listeners should, or would, be like. Readers and non-readers; speaker and listeners; teacher and disciples; to be understood or not understood; at his own time or at a later time.

Nietzsche has more to say on the character and quality of his books:

> I shall at the same time also say a word on my *art of style*. To *communicate* a state, an inner tension of pathos through signs, including the tempo of these signs — that is the meaning of every style; and considering that the multiplicity of inner states is in my case extraordinary, there exists in my case the possibility of many styles — altogether the most manifold art of style any man has ever had at his disposal. Every style is *good* which actually communicates an inner state, which makes no mistake as to the signs, the tempo of the signs, the *gestures* — all rules of phrasing are art of gesture. My instinct is here infallible. — Good style *in itself* — a piece of pure folly, mere 'idealism', on a par with the 'beautiful *in itself*', the 'good *in itself*', the 'thing *in itself*' . . . Always presupposing there are ears — that there are those capable and worthy of a similar pathos, that those are not lacking to whom one *ought* to communicate oneself. — My Zarathustra for example is at present still looking for them — alas! he will have to look for a long time yet! One has to be *worthy* of assaying him. . . And until then there will be no one who comprehends the *art* which has here been squandered. That such a thing was possible in the German language remained to be proved: I myself would previously have most hotly disputed it. Before me one

did not know what can be done with the German language
— what can be done with language as such. The art of *grand*
rhythm, the *grand style* of phrasing, as the expression of a tremendous rise and fall of sublime, or superhuman passion, was
first discovered by me; with a dithyramb such as the last of
the *third* Zarathustra, entitled 'The Seven Seals', I flew a thousand miles beyond that which has hitherto been called poesy.
(EH,74,75)

The remaining few paragraphs of "Why I Write Such Excellent
Books" returns to the distinction Nietzsche made in the opening section of "Why I Am So Wise." Father and mother, male and female,
two experiences, two apparently separate worlds. Also, two different
positions from which to view the world — two different perspectives
embedded within those experiences. And remember these words, "I
now have the skill and knowledge to *invert perspectives*: first reason
why a 'revaluation of values' is perhaps possible at all to me alone." A
revaluation into which he is embarking.

Continuing his reflecting on his books, Nietzsche adds further to
his claim of having become proficient in his ability to 'invert perspectives'. He is able to adopt the perspective of the female in addition to
that of the male — his own. And, it is the inner experiences of both in
which he is most interested. And so he writes:

That out of my writings there speaks a *psychologist* who has
not his equal, that is perhaps the first thing a good reader will
notice — a reader such as I deserve, who reads me as good old
philologists read their Horace. The propositions over which
everybody is in fundamental agreement — not to speak of everybody's philosophers, the moralists and other hollow-heads
and cabbage-heads — appear with me as naïve blunders: . . .

The Circe of mankind, morality, has falsified all *psychologica*
to its very foundations — has *moralized* it — to the point of
the frightful absurdity that love is supposed to be something
'unegoistic' . . . One has to be set firmly upon *oneself*, one has
to stand bravely upon one's own two legs, otherwise one *cannot* love at all. In the long run the little women know that all
too well: they play the deuce with selfless, with merely objective men . . . Dare I venture in addition to suggest that I
know these little women? It is part of my dionysian endowment. Who knows? perhaps I am the first psychologist of the
eternal-womanly. They all love me — an old story: excepting

the abortive women, the 'emancipated' who lack the stuff for
children. — Happily I am not prepared to be torn to pieces:
the complete woman tears to pieces when she loves . . . I know
these amiable maenads. . . . Ah, what a dangerous, creeping,
subterranean little beast of prey it is! And so pleasant with it!
. . . A little woman chasing after her revenge would over-run
fate itself. — The woman is unspeakably more wicked than
the man, also cleverer; goodness in a woman is already a form
of *degeneration*. . . At the bottom of all so-called 'beautiful souls'
there lies a physiological disadvantage — I shall not say all I
could or I should become medi-cynical. The struggle for *equal*
rights is even a symptom of sickness: every physician knows
that. — The more a woman is a woman the more she defends
herself tooth and nail against rights in general: for the state of
nature, the eternal *war* between the sexes puts her in a superior position by far. — Have there been ears for my definition
of love? it is the only one worthy of a philosopher. Love — in
its methods war, in its foundation, the mortal hatred of the
sexes. Has my answer been heard to the question how one
cures — 'redeems' — a woman? One makes a child for her.
The woman has need of children, the man is always only the
means: thus spoke Zarathustra. (*EH*,75,76)

Nietzsche ends this chapter:

To give an idea of me as a psychologist I take a curious piece
of psychology which occurs in 'Beyond Good and Evil' — I
forbid, by the way, any conjecture as to whom I am describing
in this passage: 'The genius of the heart as it is possessed by
that great hidden one, the tempter god and born pied piper
of consciences whose voice knows how to descend into the
underworld of every soul, who says no word and gives no
glance in which there lies no touch of enticement, to whose
mastery belongs knowing how to seem — not what he is but
what to those who follow him is one constraint *more* to press
ever closer to him, to follow him ever more inwardly and
thoroughly . . . The genius of the heart who makes everything
loud and self-satisfied fall silent and teaches it to listen, who
smooths rough souls and gives them a new desire to savour
— the desire to lie still as a mirror, that the deep sky may mirror itself in them . . . The genius of the heart who teaches the
stupid and hasty hand to hesitate and grasp more delicately;
who divines the hidden and forgotten treasure, the drop of
goodness and sweet spirituality under thick and opaque ice,
and is a divining-rod for every grain of gold which has laid
long in the prison of much mud and sand. . . The genius of
the heart from whose touch everyone goes away richer, not

favoured and surprised, not as if blessed and oppressed with the goods of others, but richer in himself, newer to himself than before, broken open, blown upon and sounded out by a thawing wind, more uncertain perhaps, more delicate, more fragile, more broken, but full of hopes that as yet have no names, full of new will and current, full of new ill will and counter current...' (EH,77)

Following the chapter on his books, Nietzsche takes a brief backward glance at each of his major books, in the order of the writing of each — to remember again that these books reaffirm the process of the development of his thinking. To include here a very few brief comments of his on each of these books offers an additional perspective on my interpretation of his philosophy.

On *The Birth of Tragedy*:

The book's two decisive *novelties* are, firstly the understanding of the *dionysian* phenomenon in the case of the Greeks — it offers the first psychology of this phenomenon, it sees in it the sole root of the whole of Hellenic art — . The other novelty is the understanding of Socratism: Socrates for the first time recognized as an agent of Hellenic disintegration, as a typical *decadent*. 'Rationality' *against* instinct. 'Rationality' at any price as dangerous, as a force undermining life! ...

This beginning is remarkable beyond all measure. I had *discovered* the only likeness and parallel to my own innermost experience which history possesses — I had therewith become the first to comprehend the wonderful phenomenon of the dionysian. (EH,79)

On *The Untimely Essays*:

THE four *untimely essays* are altogether warlike. They demonstrate that I was no 'Jack o' Dreams', that I derive pleasure from drawing the sword — also, perhaps, that I have a dangerously supple wrist. The *first* attack (1873) was on German culture, which even at that time I already looked down on with remorseless contempt. ....

The *second* untimely essay (1874) brings to light what is dangerous, what gnaws at and poisons life, in our way of carrying on science — : life sick with this inhuman clockwork and mechanism, with the 'impersonality' of the worker, with the

false economy of 'division of labour'. The *goal* gets lost, culture
— the means, the modern way of carrying on science, *barba-
rized* ... In this essay the 'historical sense' of which this century is so proud is recognized for the first time as a sickness, as a
typical sign of decay. — In the *third* and *fourth* untimely essays
two pictures of the sternest *selfishness, self-discipline* are erected
against this, as signposts to a *higher* concept of culture, to the
restoration of the concept 'culture': ...

What I am today, *where* I am today — at a height at which I no
longer speak with words but with lightning bolts — oh how
far away I was from it in those days! But I *saw* the land — I did
not deceive myself for a moment as to the way, sea, danger —
and success! (*EH*,84,87)

On *Human, All Too Human*:

'HUMAN, All Too Human' is the memorial of a crisis. It calls
itself a book for *free* spirits: almost every sentence in it is the
expression of a victory — with this book I liberated myself
from that in my nature which *did not belong to me*. Idealism does
not belong to me: the title says: 'where *you* see ideal things, *I*
see — humans, alas all too human things!' ... I know humanity *better*. ...

It is a war, but a war without powder and smoke, without
warlike attitudes, without pathos and contorted limbs — all
this would still have been 'idealism'. ...

A downright burning thirst seized hold of me: thenceforward
I pursued in fact nothing other than physiology, medicine and
natural science — I returned to actual historical studies only
when the *task* compelled me to. ...

But in any event as a proposition with the weightiest consequences, at once fruitful and fearful and looking out at the
world with the *Janus-face* possessed by all great perceptions. ..
(*EH*,89,90,91,92,94)

On *Daybreak*:

WITH this book begins my campaign against morality. Not
that it smells in the slightest of gunpowder — quite other and
more pleasant odours will be perceived in it, provided one has
some subtlety in one's nostrils. ..

The question of the origin of moral values is therefore for me a question of the *first rank* because it conditions the future of mankind. . .

When one directs seriousness away from self-preservation, enhancement of bodily strength, when one makes of green-sickness an ideal, of contempt for the body 'salvation of the soul', what else is it but a *recipe* for *decadence*? — Loss of cen-tre of gravity, resistance to the natural instincts, in a word 'selflessness' — that has hitherto been called *morality*. . . With 'Daybreak' I first took up the struggle against the morality of unselfing. — (*EH*,95,96,97)

On *The Gay Science*:

'DAYBREAK' is an affirmative book, profound but bright and benevolent. The same applies once again and in the highest degree to the *gaya scienza*: in practically every sentence of this book profundity and exuberance go hand in hand. (*EH*,98)

On *Thus Spoke Zarathustra*:

I SHALL now tell the story of Zarathustra. The basic concep-tion of the work, the *idea of eternal recurrence*, the highest for-mula of affirmation that can possibly be attained — belongs to the August of the year 1881: it was jotted down on a piece of paper with the inscription: '6,000 feet beyond man and time'. I was that day walking through the woods beside the lake of Silvaplana; I stopped beside a mighty pyramidal block of stone which reared itself up not far from Surlei. Then this idea came to me. — If I reckon a couple of months back from this day I find as an omen a sudden and profoundly decisive altera-tion in my taste, above all in music. The whole of Zarathustra might perhaps be reckoned as music; — certainly a rebirth of the art of *hearing* was a precondition of it. . .

The text, I may state expressly because a misunderstanding exists about it, is not by me: it is the astonishing inspiration of a young Russian lady with whom I was then friendly, Frau-lein Lou von Salome. . .

The *body* is inspired: let us leave the 'soul' out of it . . . I could often have been seen dancing; at that time I could walk for seven or eight hours in the mountains without a trace of tiredness. I slept well, I laughed a lot — I was perfectly vigor-ous and perfectly patient. . .

The ladder upon which he climbs up and down is tremendous; he has seen further, willed further, *been able* further than
any other human being. He contradicts with every word, this
most affirmative of all spirits; all opposites are in him bound
together into a new unity. The highest and the lowest forces
of human nature, the sweetest, most frivolous and most fearsome stream forth out of *one* fountain with immortal certainty. Until then one does not know what height, what depth
is; one knows even less what truth is. There is no moment in
this revelation of truth which would have been anticipated
or divined by even *one* of the greatest. There is no wisdom, no
psychology, no art of speech before Zarathustra: the nearest
things, the most everyday things here speak of things unheard
of.

It is precisely this compass of space, in this access to opposites that Zarathustra feels himself to be the *highest species of all
existing things*, . . .

But that is the concept of Dionysos himself.—Another consideration
leads to the same conclusion. The psychological problem in
the type of Zarathustra is how he, to an unheard of degree
says No, *does* No to everything to which one has hitherto
said Yes, can nonetheless be the opposite of a spirit of denial;
how he, a spirit bearing the heaviest of destinies, a fatality
of a task, can nonetheless be the lightest and most opposite
— Zarathustra is a dancer — : how he, who has the harshest, the most fearful insight into reality, who has thought the
'most abysmal thought', nonetheless finds in it no objection
to existence, nor even to the eternal recurrence of existence
— rather one more reason *to be himself* the eternal Yes to all
things, 'the tremendous unbounded Yes and Amen'. . . 'Into
every abyss I still hear the blessing of my affirmation'. . . *But
that is the concept of Dionysos once more. . .*

On one occasion Zarathustra strictly defines his task — it is
also mine — the *meaning* of which cannot be misunderstood:
he is *affirmative* to the point of justifying, or redeeming even
the entire past. . .

Among the decisive preconditions for a *dionysian* task is
the hardness of the hammer, *joy even in destruction*. The imperative 'become hard', the deepest *certainty that all creators are hard*, is the actual mark of a dionysian nature.
— (*EH*,99,100,104,106,107,110,111)

On *Beyond Good and Evil*:

THE task for the immediately following years was as clear as it could be. Now that the affirmative part of my task was done, it was the turn of the denying, the No-saying and *No-doing* part: the revaluation of existing values themselves, the great war — the evocation of a day of decision. Included here is the slow search for those related to me, for such as out of strength would offer me their hand for *the work of destruction.* — From now on all my writings are fish-hooks: perhaps I understand fishing as well as anyone?. . . If nothing got *caught* I am not to blame. *There were no fish.* . .

This book (1886) is in all essentials a *critique of modernity,* . . .

The eye grown through a tremendous compulsion accustomed to seeing *afar* — Zarathustra is more farsighted even than the Tsar — is here constrained to focus sharply on what is close at hand, the age, what is *around us.* . . .

Refinement in form, in intention, in the art of *keeping silent,* is in the foreground, psychology is employed with an avowed harshness and cruelty — there is not a single good-natured word in the entire book. . . (EH,112,113)

On *Genealogy of Morals*:

THE three essays of which this Genealogy consists are in regard to expression, intention and art of surprise perhaps the uncanniest things that have ever been written. Dionysos is, as one knows, also the god of darkness. — Each time a beginning which is *intended* to mislead, cool, scientific, even ironic, intentionally foreground, intentionally keeping in suspense. Gradually an increasing disquiet; isolated flashes of lightning; very unpleasant truths becoming audible as a dull rumbling in the distance — until at last a *tempo feroce* is attained in which everything surges forward with tremendous tension. At the conclusion each time amid perfectly awful detonations a *new* truth visible between thick clouds. — The truth of the *first* essay is the psychology of Christianity: the birth of Christianity out of the spirit of *ressentiment, not,* as is no doubt believed, out of the 'spirit' — essentially a counter-movement, the great revolt against the domination of *noble* values. The *second* essay gives the psychology of the *conscience*: it is *not,* as is no doubt believed, 'the voice of God in man' — it is the instinct of cruelty turned backwards after it can no longer discharge itself outwards. Cruelty here brought to light for the first time as one of the oldest substrata of culture and one that can least be thought away. The *third* essay gives the answer to the question where the tremendous *power* of the ascetic ideal, the priestly ideal, comes from, although it is the *harmful* ideal *par excellence*, a will to the end, a *decadence* ideal. Answer: *not* because God is active behind the priests, which is no doubt believed, but *faute de mieux* — because hitherto it has been the only ideal, because it had no competitors. 'For man will rather will nothingness than *not* will'. . . What was lacking above was a *counter-ideal — until the advent of Zarathustra.*—I have been understood. Three decisive preliminary studies of a psychologist for a revaluation of all values. — This book contains the first psychology of the priest. (*EH*,114,115)

On *Twilight of the Idols*:

THIS writing of fewer than 150 pages, cheerful and fateful in tone, a demon which laughs — the work of so few days I hesitate to reveal their number, is the exception among books: there exists nothing more rich in substance, more independent, more overthrowing — more wicked. If you want to get a quick idea of how everything was upsidedown before me, make a start with this writing. That which is called *idol* on the title-page is quite simply that which has hitherto been called truth. *Twilight of the Idols* — in plain terms: the old truth is coming to an end. . . (*EH*,116)

On *The Wagner Case*:

IF one is to be fair to this writing one has to suffer from the destiny of music as from an open wound. — *What* is it I suffer from when I suffer from the destiny of music? From this: that music has been deprived of its world-transfiguring, affirmative character, that it is *decadence* music and no longer the flute of Dionysos. . . (*EH*,119)

PART ELEVEN

In reading the last chapter of *Ecce Homo*, "Why I Am A Destiny," one has the sense that Nietzsche was in the process of fully realizing where his philosophical journey had been taking him, and that indeed, this was the place. There is almost the need here, for us the readers, to reproduce the entire chapter. However, instead we will follow his footsteps as carefully as possible.

Almost from the beginning of his writing, Nietzsche posted notices throughout that he was playing with fire, that he was deadly serious, and should be recognized as dangerous. But intermingling with this seriousness, he reminded us throughout that he was playful, a trickster, even a buffoon, skilled in the art of illusion. He made clear that he was a lover of puzzles, riddles, conundrums of every sort — both as a solver and as a creator. His awareness of the frightful potential of his own thinking, which he nevertheless believed must be spoken, led him to this, "You see I do my best to be understood with difficulty."

Given Nietzsche's directions, it would be folly to consider him otherwise. His writings are as he described them — many puzzles and many riddles. Here near the final stages of his intense life — wise, clever, writer of excellent books — his last chapter of *Ecce Homo* appears to condense all prior puzzles into 'The Puzzle'. And he would add, "he sees the target, and perhaps has the arrows." And the target? Christian morality.

From the beginning:

> I KNOW my fate. One day there will be associated with my name the recollection of something frightful — of a crisis like no other before on earth, of the profoundest collision of con- science, of a decision evoked *against* everything that until then had been believed in, demanded, sanctified. I am not a man I am dynamite. — And with all that there is nothing in me of a founder of a religion — religions are affairs of the rabble, I have need of washing my hands after contact with religious people. . . I do not *want* 'believers', I think I am too malicious to believe in myself, I never speak to masses. . . I have a ter- rible fear I shall one day be pronounced *holy*: one will guess why I bring out this book *beforehand*; it is intended to prevent people from making mischief with me . . . I do not want to be a saint, rather even a buffoon . . . Perhaps I am a buffoon . . . And nonetheless, or rather *not* nonetheless — for there has hith- erto been nothing more mendacious than saints — the truth speaks out of me. — But my truth is *dreadful*: for hitherto the *lie* has been called truth. — *Revaluation of all values*: this is my formula for an act of supreme coming-to-oneself on the part of mankind which in me has become flesh and genius. It is my fate to have to be the first *decent* human being, to know myself in opposition to the mendaciousness of millennia . . . I was the first to *discover* the truth, in that I was the first to sense — *smell* — the lie as lie . . . My genius is in my nostrils. . . I contra- dict as has never been contradicted and am nonetheless the opposite of a negative spirit. I am a *bringer of good tidings* such as there has never been, I know tasks from such a height that any conception of them has hitherto been lacking; only after me is it possible to hope again. With all that I am necessarily a man of fatality. For when truth steps into battle with the lie of millennia we shall have convulsions, an earthquake spasm, a transposition of valley and mountain such as has never been dreamed of. The concept politics has then become completely absorbed into a war of spirits, all the power-structures of the old society have been blown into the air — they one and all reposed on the lie: there will be wars such as there have never yet been on earth. Only after me will there be *grand politics* on earth. — (*EH*,126,127)

'Yes' and 'no', truth and lie, but here in his 'last testament' a reaf- firmation of what, in some fundamental sense, had been at stake from the beginning — *power*. "I am not a man I am dynamite." ". . . all the power-structures of the old society have been blown into the air — they all reposed on the lie." Nietzsche's philosophy is a philosophy of power — *human power*. And we should understand immediately that human power, or powers, so simply, means male powers and female powers. And importantly, it means the powers involved in saying 'yes' and saying 'no'. In these last few pages of his summary of a lifetime, he would have had to assume that his cherished readers would have been familiar with the central role power always plays in human life, in human experience, and in his philosophy. And at this point we need to remember. However, a fuller account is needed and will come later.

In "Why I Am A Destiny," Nietzsche continues:

> I am by far the most terrible human being there has ever been; this does not mean I shall not be the most beneficent. I know joy in *destruction* to a degree corresponding to my *strength* for destruction — in both I obey my dionysian nature, which does not know how to separate No-doing from Yes-saying. I am the first *immoralist*: I am therewith the *destroyer par excellence*.— (EH,127)

Nietzsche is saying 'No' to morality, or to being a moralist, and 'Yes' to immorality, or to being an immoralist. Before we are finished it will become necessary to revisit this pair of opposites. Here, just this reminder as to what he is determined to destroy. Nietzsche defines morality (a definition that needs to be memorized):

> — morality understood as the doctrine of the rank-relations that produce the phenomenon we call "life." — (BGE,22)

Continuing in this concluding chapter of his last book:

> I have not been asked, as I should have been asked, what the name Zarathustra means in precisely my mouth, in the mouth of the first immoralist: for what constitutes the tremendous uniqueness of that Persian in history is precisely the opposite of this. Zarathustra was the first to see in the struggle be-

tween good and evil the actual wheel in the working of things: the translation of morality into the realm of metaphysics, as force, cause, end-in-itself, is *his* work. But this question is itself at bottom its own answer. Zarathustra *created* this most fateful of errors, morality: consequently he must also be the first to *recognize* it. Not only has he had longer and greater experience here than any other thinker — the whole of history is indeed the experimental refutation of the proposition of a so-called 'moral world-order' — : what is more important is that Zarathustra is more truthful than any other thinker. His teaching, and his alone, upholds truthfulness as the supreme virtue — that is to say, the opposite of the *cowardice* of the 'idealist', who takes flight in face of reality; Zarathustra has more courage in him than all other thinkers put together. To tell the truth and *to shoot well with arrows*: that is Persian virtue. — Have I been understood? The self-overcoming of morality through truthfulness, the self-overcoming of the moralist into his opposite — *into me* — that is what the name Zarathustra means in my mouth. (*EH*,127,128)

Good and evil — the opposites which Nietzsche reserves for the basic element of morality. This last passage qualifies as one of Nietzsche's last puzzles — or as one major part of his last puzzle. Zarathustra, the Persian, was the first to claim the struggle between good and evil as the defining force in the universe, but his meaning was one that was abstract, metaphysical — good versus evil "in itself". For him, this was the ultimate dualism, the eternal conflict of opposites, governing human beings.

Zarathustra, the Nietzschean, was the first to deny the abstract, metaphysical notions of good and evil, and the first to recognize this conflict of opposites in human affairs, or human experience. Nietzsche, or Nietzsche's Zarathustra, with great experience living with this morality — this conflict, this 'doctrine of rank-relations' — made it his task to 'overcome morality'.

Nietzsche's torturously labyrinthine journey had led him to these "open seas". Not only had morality, especially Christian morality, been invented as a doctrine of the rank, the power, and the value of the male/father over the rank, the power, and the value of the female/ mother. That morality, or hierarchical arrangement, had assigned the idea, and word "good" to the male, and the idea, and word "evil" to the female. Man became "good", woman became "evil". Nietzsche had set out to interpret or understand, to evaluate, to expose, and to destroy this hierarchical relationship of power, value, and rank. Of all the words used to describe what he had become, "immoralist" took on the defining aspect. And his " revaluation of all values" was directed first of all toward this destructive form of valuing — morality. To change the world, change the way in which humans value people — males and females — as well as other values.

In Section four of "Why I Am A Destiny," Nietzsche continues:

> At bottom my expression *immoralist* involves two denials. I deny first a type of man who has hitherto counted as the highest, the *good*, the *benevolent*, the *beneficent*; I deny secondly a kind of morality which has come to be accepted and to dominate as morality in itself — *decadent* morality, in more palpable terms *Christian* morality. The second contradiction might be seen as the decisive one, since the over-evaluation of goodness and benevolence by and large already counts with me as a consequence of *decadence*, as a symptom of weakness, as incompatible with an ascending and affirmative life: denial *and destruction* is a condition of affirmation. — I deal first of all with the psychology of the good man. In order to assess what a type of man is worth one has to compute how much his preservation costs — one has to know the conditions of his existence. The condition for the existence of the good is the *lie* — : expressed differently, the *desire* not to see at any price what is the fundamental constitution of reality, that is to say *not* such as to call forth benevolent instincts at all times, even less such as to permit at all times an interference by short-sighted good-natured hands. . .
>
> Zarathustra, the first to grasp that optimism is just as decadent as pessimism and perhaps more harmful, says: good men never tell the truth. The good taught you false shores and false securities: you were born and kept in the lies of the good. Everything has been distorted and twisted down to its very bottom through the good. . .
>
> In this sense Zarathustra calls the good now 'the ultimate men', now the 'beginning of the end'; above all he feels them to be the *most harmful species of man*, because they preserve their existence as much at the expense of *truth* as at the expense of the *future*. . .
>
> The good — have always been the beginning of the end. . .

And whatever harm the world-calumniators may do, *the harm the good do is the most harmful harm.* (*EH*,128,129,130)

Nietzsche began *Ecce Homo* by saying simply and unequivocally that humanity is divided into two types — females and males. Everything which he says after that may be understood as additional interpretations relating to that pair of opposites. Every distinction, every difference, to which he gives attention — directly or indirectly, literally or metaphorically — is to echo this dualism, and to explore further the dynamics of power which has always existed, and recurs eternally.

From the beginning of *Ecce Homo*, Nietzsche is building to the climax, to this last chapter. He is still caught in the contradictory desires — to be understood and not to be understood. To expose his thinking and at the same time to withhold those thoughts which he knows are fearsome — even to himself.

Increasingly the major contraries which Nietzsche reasserts are becoming denial and affirmation, creation and destruction, good and evil, morality and immorality, power and weakness, and perhaps topping them all, truth and lie. But all of these, as well as many others of lesser significance, are constantly in play.

Section Five of "Why I Am A Destiny" again calls upon Nietzsche's Zarathustra. It begins:

> Zarathustra, the first psychologist of the good, is — consequently — a friend of the wicked. When a *decadence*-species of man has risen to the rank of the highest species of man, this can happen only at the expense of its antithetical species, the species of man strong and certain of life. When the herd-animal is resplendent in the glow of the highest virtue, the exceptional man must be devalued to the wicked man. (*EH*,130)

Pause here. Nietzsche is "the first psychologist of the good." He has delved deeply into his own psyche, his own consciousness, and the psyche of others of the same type — males. And he has discovered and uncovered some long-buried or concealed phenomena. Chief among these is resentment, and the "desire not to see at any price what is the fundamental constitution of reality" — the *lie*, which is the "condition of the existence of the good."

Continue. Zarathustra "is — consequently — a friend of the wicked." The result which followed from Nietzsche becoming "the first psychologist of the good" is that he responded by becoming a "friend of the wicked." And the word "wicked" is rich in possible meanings — typical of much that one has to remember in unravelling his puzzles. He is again contrasting the "good" male and the "evil" female. "Wicked" may mean — "morally very bad, evil; disposed to, or marked by mischief; disgustingly unpleasant; causing, or likely to cause, harm, distress, trouble; goes beyond reasonable or predictable limits; of exceptional quality or degree." Remember that earlier in the book Nietzsche had written, "Who knows? Perhaps I am the first psychologist of the eternal-womanly." And the woman has been called "wicked"?

Section Five continues:

> It is at this point and nowhere else that one must make a start if one is to understand what Zarathustra's intentions are: the species of man he delineates delineates reality *as it is*: he is strong enough for it — he is not estranged from or entranced by it, he is *reality itself*, he still has all that is fearful and questionable in reality in him, *only thus can man possess greatness. . .* (EH,130)

Again, Nietzsche follows wherever the binary-opposition leads. One species, mankind — consisting of two species, or types. Zarathustra has carefully delineated a "new" species, Nietzsche's "superman", who has the courage to see reality — nature, life, sexuality, himself — as it really is, and to speak the truth. To say an unqualified "yes" to life, to overcome ressentiment, to revalue himself.

In Section Six of "Why I Am A Destiny," Nietzsche returned to the word "immoralist" and to himself as an "immoralist," The entire short section actually is putting into a few short sentences the subject to which he has given much of his energy. It reads:

But there is also another sense in which I have chosen for my-self the word *immoralist* as a mark of distinction and badge of honour; I am proud to possess the word which sets me off against the whole of humanity. No one has yet felt *Christian* morality as *beneath* him: that requires a height, a farsighted-ness, a hitherto altogether unheard-of psychological profun-dity and abysmalness. Christian morality has hitherto been the Circe of all thinkers — they stood in its service. — Who before me has entered the caverns out of which the poisonous blight of this kind of ideal — *world-calumny!* — wells up? Who has even ventured to suspect *that* these caverns exist? Who before me at all among philosophers has been a *psychologist* and not rather its opposite 'higher swindler', 'idealist'? Before me there was no psychology. — To be the first here can be a curse, it is in any case a destiny: *for one is also the first to despise. . . Disgust* at mankind is my danger. . . (*EH*,131)

In Nietzsche's lexicon, morality means "the doctrine of rank-re-lations that produce the phenomenon we call 'life'." Christian moral-ity unmistakably and unquestionably ranks the male/father as being superior and dominant in relation to the inferior and submissive fe-male/mother. Nietzsche refers to Christian morality as "the poison-ous blight" of this idea, or 'ideal'.

The remainder of "Why I AM A Destiny," in his own accounting, is Nietzsche's final plea, his final cry, his final putting into his own words, who he has become and what his philosophical creations have been. What follows are passages from Section Seven:

Have I been understood? — What defines me, what sets me apart from all the rest of mankind, is that I have unmasked Christian morality. . .

Blindness in the face of Christianity is the *crime par excellence* — the crime *against life.* . .

Christian morality — the most malicious form of the will to the lie, the actual Circe of mankind: that which has *ruined* it. It is *not* error as error which horrifies me at the sight of this, *not* the millennia-long lack of 'good will', of discipline, of de-cency, of courage in spiritual affairs which betrays itself in its victory — it is the lack of nature, it is the utterly ghastly fact that *anti-nature* itself has received the highest honours as morality, and has hung over mankind as law, as categorical imperative! . . . To blunder to this extent, *not* as an individual, *not* as a people, but as mankind! . . . That contempt has been taught for the primary instincts of life; that a 'soul', a 'spirit' has been *lyingly invented* in order to destroy the body; that one teaches that there is something unclean in the precondition of life, sexuality; . . . (EH,131,132)

The use of the word "immoralist" has been adopted by Nietzsche as a word which would probably challenge everyone. He intends to arouse interest, to be perplexing, in order to use this response by others as an opportunity to point out that everyone appears to have resolved to close their eyes, to become blind in looking at Christianity. He is endeavoring to open eyes, change perspectives, raise consciousness. The essential character of Christian morality — that to which everyone appears to be blind — is that this morality is *anti-nature* — and that means that Christianity is *anti-life, anti-body, anti-sexuality*, and more. Nietzsche's criticism is not that Christianity is an error, but rather it is a *lie*.

The direction in which Nietzsche's thinking was being propelled was revealed in this short fragment written in his late twenties. It needs to be remembered. From a piece entitled "Homer's Contest," Nietzsche wrote:

> When one speaks of *humanity*, the idea is fundamental that this is something which separates and distinguishes man from nature. In reality, however, there is no such separation: "natural" qualities, and those called truly "human" are inseparably grown together. Man in his highest and noblest capacities, is wholly nature and embodies its uncanny dual character. Those of his abilities which are terrifying and considered inhuman may even be the fertile soil out of which alone all humanity can grow in impulse, deed, and work. (PN,32)

In believing that *Ecce Homo* may be considered as the summary of Nietzsche's philosophical position, we need to look backward to additional thinking he had done regarding nature. Just as Nietzsche considered that by calling himself an "immoralist" the question would be raised as to what *he* meant by "moralist", or "morality", by calling Christianity "anti-nature" I think he intended for the question to be raised as to what *he* meant by "nature". Or to why this had become of such interest to him. And these questions have been raised by several of his interpreters and critics. Rather than add his voice to those beginning to challenge Christianity on the basis of its being non-rational, Nietzsche chose to redirect attention and awareness that Christianity was "anti-nature".

I think that either of these two possible meanings may be close to what Nietzsche had in mind. First, nature may be defined as "the universe with all its phenomena, i.e. all objects of awareness in experience." Second, nature may mean "the sum total of the forces at work throughout the universe, or world." Nietzsche had his own way of interpreting and expressing the meaning of the world, or *nature*. In a passage written in 1885, which remained unpublished, but which was printed by the editors of *Will to Power*, Nietzsche wrote this:

> And do you know what 'the world' is to me? Shall I show it to you in my mirror? This world: a monster of energy, without beginning, without end; an immovable, brazen enormity of energy, which does not grow bigger or smaller, which does not expend itself but only transforms itself; as a whole of unalterable size, a household without expenses or losses, but likewise without increase or income; enclosed by 'nothingness' as by a boundary; not something flowing away or squandering itself, not something endlessly extended, but as a definite quantity of energy set in a definite space and not a space that might be 'empty' here or there, but rather as energy throughout, as a play of energies and waves of energy at the same time one and many, increasing here and at the same time decreasing there; a sea of energies flowing and rushing together, eternally moving, eternally flooding back, with tremendous years of recurrence, with an ebb and flow of its forms; out of the simplest forms striving towards the most complex, out of the stillest, most rigid, coldest form toward the hottest, most turbulent, most self-contradictory, and then out of this abundance returning home to the simple, out of the play of contradiction back to the joy of unison, still affirming itself in the uniformity of its courses and its years, blessing itself as that which must return eternally, as a becoming that knows no repletion, no satiety, no weariness — : this is my *Dionysian* world of the eternally self-creative, the eternally self-destructive, this mystery world of the twofold delight, this my 'beyond good and evil', without aim, unless the joy of the circle is itself an aim; without will, unless a ring feeling goodwill towards itself — do you want a *name* for this world? A *solution* for all your riddles? A *light* for you too, you best con-

cealed, strongest, most dismayed, most midnight men? — *This world is the will to power — and nothing beside!* And you yourself are also this will to power — and nothing beside! (N,136)

Nature, the world, is a "monster of energy." Could the basic char-acter of nature have been described more practically, more accu-rately, more eloquently, offering more unforeseen possibilities for the future? And in placing mankind back into nature, Nietzsche names this human energy "the will to power." Humans belong to nature, participate in nature. Life, all life, is the will to power. This is the fundamental fact of all life. Nature throughout, everywhere, all the time, is energy, power. Power belongs to nature, nature *is* power. The transfer of ultimate power to the Christian god, in Nietzsche's inter-pretation, constituted an intentional *lie*.

Nietzsche's philosophy may be called a philosophy of natural-ism, or *nature*, and at the same time, a philosophy of *power*. His theory of nature is developed on the basis of two propositions. First, "Man in his highest and noblest capacities, is wholly nature and embodies its uncanny dual character." Second, *"This world is the will to power — and nothing beside! And you yourself are also this will to power — and nothing beside!"*

In his first major book, in 1878, Nietzsche was already beginning to think about most of the major issues or problems which he would include in his final philosophical position. Especially obvious are Christianity, deception, good and evil, honesty, lies, morality, nature, power, revenge, self-deception, truth, woman, and many others. On the treatment of Nietzsche's philosophy of power, one of the fore-most Nietzsche scholars, R. J. Hollingdale, in my view, is the best, or at least is my favorite. His extensive elucidation of the development of Nietzsche's thinking on power in his book, *Nietzsche*, is valuable. For my purposes here, I borrow a few of Hollingdale's important highlights.

> To grasp Nietzsche's theory of will to power and its ramifica-tions one cannot do better than trace the idea as it appears at this or that place in his works and see how it formed itself into a hypothesis which was then consciously employed, con-

sistently yet still experimentally as an explanatory principle.
But perhaps it would help to provide a sense of direction to
look first at the end result and the final formulation. Near the
beginning of *The Anti-Christ* we find the following series of
questions and answers:

'What is good? — All that heightens the feeling of power, the
will to power, power itself in man. What is bad? — All that
proceeds from weakness. What is happiness? — The feeling
that power *increases* — that a resistance is overcome' (A,2)

The abruptness and uncompromisingness of these assertions
are characteristic of the works of 1888: they are a condensation
of the sense and purpose of the whole 'philosophy of power'
as it has been built up during the course of years. 'Goodness'
and 'happiness' are identified: what is good is what heightens
the feeling of power, happiness is this feeling itself, which can
be experienced only in the form of the feeling of *more* power.
(N,76)

Nietzsche suggests, and then elaborates on this notion. Humans
are conscious of the feeling of power, and *all* actions are prompted
by the desire, the impulse, the drive for the subjective sensation of
increased power. In commenting further, Hollingdale says:

What he appears to say is that the drive to enhanced power
is, as a matter of fact, the basic drive in man, and the feeling
of enhanced power the becoming-conscious of the successful
operation of this drive: mankind desires only greater power
and is consequently happy when, and only when, this desire
is satisfied. (N,87)

However, although the manifestations of the power-drive, in
themselves, always are accompanied by the feeling of power, and
are experienced as "good"; and although the feeling that power is increasing is Nietzsche's interpretation of happiness, the psychology of
this drive and this feeling are much more complex. In *The Gay Science*
Nietzsche wrote this:

On the doctrine of the feeling of power. — Benefiting and hurting
others are ways of exercising one's power over others; that

is all one desires in such cases. One hurts those whom one wants to feel one's power, for pain is a much more efficient means to that end than pleasure; pain always raises the question about its origin while pleasure is inclined to stop with itself without looking back . . . Certainly the state in which we hurt others is rarely as agreeable, in an unadulterated way, as that in which we benefit others; it is a sign that we are still lacking power, or it shows a sense of frustration in the face of this poverty; it is accompanied by new dangers and uncertainties for what power we do possess, and clouds our horizon with the prospect of revenge, scorn, punishment and failure. (GS,86,87)

Hollingdale adds this:

. . . for all history and all private experience provides evidence that there is at any rate *something* men, women and animals desire more than they desire the simple continuation of life, and for the sake of which they are willing to risk life. Nietzsche's innovation is to suggest that this something — which unquestionably exists — is the feeling of enhanced power — and he ventures the generalization that it is the drive to attain this feeling which lies behind all activity. (N,91)

Nietzsche insists repeatedly that life is a contest, or conflict. His view is that conflict is a general, necessary condition of life, which is accounted for by the ubiquity of the will to power. This drive for power, which defines every human life, may be directed toward oneself or toward others. In great detail and in unexpected situations, Nietzsche attempts to account for a large range of human actions which proceed from a single source. All have their origin from some aspect of the possession of, or the drive to maintain, or the desire to enhance power. There is one single basic motive, shared by all persons.

The energy, or power, of nature is manifested as creative, generative, productive and as destructive. Humans, as embodiments of power, do likewise. As conscious human beings, we create new human creatures, new life, new embodiments of energy, or power. We create what we are — one's self. We create words, names, images, definitions, meanings, speech, art, inventions, knowledge, laws, ideas, lies, and most important — values.

And *we* destroy, exercising, or expressing the will to power. The process of nature is a constant dialectic between the powers of creating and the powers of destroying, recreating, and renewing. This dynamic with humans is embodied, personalized, often becomes intense, bitter, severe. The feeling of increased power is accompanied by intervals of the negative aspect, that is the feeling of impotence, of weakness, of fear.

In further elaborating on Nietzsche's interpretation that will to power is the basic psychological drive in humans, Hollingdale recognizes another psychological phenomenon to which Nietzsche gave special attention. He writes this:

> What is desired, according to this theory, is the feeling of increased power. The negative aspect, that is to say the feeling of impotence, of being subject to the power of another, produces as its characteristic effect the phenomenon of *ressentiment* — and this is the chief corollary of the theory of will to power. Nietzsche developed the psychology of resentment almost as luxuriently [sic] as he did that of power: the essence of it is that the powerless man feels resentment against those whose power he feels and against this state of powerlessness itself and out of this feeling of resentment *takes revenge* — on other people or on life itself. The objective of the revenge is to get rid of the feeling of powerlessness:.... (N,183)

No thinker has been more conscious of this dynamics of power and weakness, of creating and destroying, than Nietzsche. And, one may claim that no other thinker has become more intellectually and emotionally involved in probing and exposing the process than he did.

As Nietzsche was developing his philosophy of power, the evidence in his writings suggests that he was discovering that possibly he was in pursuit of the most complex, resistant phenomenon in human experience — that energy, or power, *was* something of a "monster." Elusive, constantly changing forms, ebbing and flowing, eternally moving, increasing here and at the same time decreasing there, a sea flowing and rushing together. A solution for all your riddles? Or, the ever-present, ultimate riddle itself?

In human experiences, the desire for the feeling of power — to acquire, to maintain, to increase — manifests itself possibly in endless ways or situations. No claim is being made here of solving, or resolving, the riddle of power — what it means, who exercises it, in what forms, etc. But Nietzsche would urge that we persist with the questions, to further pursue those concerns related to positions of power, relations of power, structures of power, the uses and abuses of power.

The many meanings, or manifestations, of power appear to fall into two clusters, with different emphases. One group includes these — authority, jurisdiction, control, command, dominion — suggesting the *right* to govern, rule, determine, dominate. Another group includes these — energy, force, strength, might — suggesting the *ability* to exert effort, and may imply the latent, or exerted, physical or mental ability to act or produce an effect. Nietzsche recognized and addressed all of these. He himself particularly had the *power* — the energy, the ability, to destroy old ideas and to create new ideas and words, to influence others with the power of his words.

More than any thinker before him, Nietzsche became aware of the power attached to speech, of the power manifested by those *who* speak, and the corresponding lack of power, or weakness, of those *who* do not speak, who are excluded from speech. And also of those who have spoken in the past, and those who have not spoken. He wrote this:

> *Only as creators!* — This has given me the greatest trouble and still does: to realize that what things are *called* is incomparably more important than what they are. The reputation, name, and appearance, the usual measure and weight of a thing, what it counts for — originally almost always wrong and arbitrary, thrown over things like a dress and altogether foreign to their nature and even to their skin—all this grows from generation unto generation, merely because people believe in it, until it gradually grows to be part of the thing and turns into its very body. What at first was appearance becomes in the end, almost invariably, the essence and is effective as such. How foolish it would be to suppose that one only needs to point out this origin and this misty shroud of delusion in order to *destroy* the world that counts for real, so-called "*reality*."

We can destroy only as creators. — But let us not forget this either: it is enough to create new names and estimations and probabilities in order to create in the long run new 'things'. (*GS*,121,122)

As natural creatures, human beings exercise power in creating new creatures, new life, new embodiments of power. In becoming conscious, the greatest, most powerful display of human power is that of *speech*. Humans create images, models, laws. Most important, in manifesting the power of words, humans create *values* — and thereby a world. Nietzsche wrote this:

> We who think and feel at the same time are those who really continually *fashion* something that had not been there before: the whole eternally growing world of valuations, colors, accents, perspectives, scales, affirmations, and negations. . . Whatever has value in our world does not have value in itself, according to its nature — nature is always value-less, but has been given value at some time, as a present — and it was *we* who gave and bestowed it. Only we have created the world *that concerns man*! But precisely this knowledge we lack, and when we occasionally catch it for a fleeting moment we always forget it again immediately; we fail to recognize our best power and underestimate ourselves, the contemplatives, just a little. We are *neither as proud nor as happy* as we might be. (*GS*,241,242)

In the eternally growing and changing world of valuations, we humans are continually creating and destroying values — with the power of words, of speech. Nature is energy, or power, throughout, including natural creatures. However, in Nietzsche's thinking, "nature is always value-less. . . Only we have created the world *that concerns man*!" What does it mean to be human? It means that humans are inextricably creatures of nature, while at the same time we are the creators of another world within the natural world. Our "best power," other than the power of creating new life, is the power of creating new values — through the power of words.

Power and value also are inextricably interconnected, and questions to be asked are always questions by humans about humans.

Who has value? Who creates, or has in the past, created values? Who creates, or determines, a table of values, a ranking order of values? Humans create and destroy values. We also create and destroy any ranking of values. Nature is always rank-less, as well as value-less. And power and rank are also inextricably interconnected. These three — power, value, and rank — are inextricably interconnected, or interrelated. In Nietzsche's words, "What determines your rank is the quantum of power you are. . ." In nature, hierarchies do not exist.

Nietzsche appears to agree with an earlier interpretation of Thomas Hobbes that power is the standard of value when valuing people. In establishing what Nietzsche refers to as a "table of values," it is first *who* is valued, next which *actions* are valued, and then what *things* are valued (like "small things"). There is this reminder from *Beyond Good and Evil*:

> It is obvious that the moral value-characteristics are at first applied to *people* and only later, in a transferred sense, to acts. (*BGE*,203)

Values, especially moral values, or morality, are at the heart of Nietzsche's critique of Christianity. Christianity had been invented, brought into existence, for the purpose of changing the world, by changing the values — primarily the moral values. It was designed and developed to create a new order of powers and values. The power of the Christian religion was, and had been, the power of establishing and enforcing the morality which ranked the value and power of the male above the value and power of the female.

Nietzsche became a self-proclaimed, avowed *immoralist*, and he set himself the task of exposing, and declaring his war of words against Christian morality. It had revealed itself to be a disaster. Continuing in Section Seven of *Ecce Homo*, speaking still of Christian morality, Nietzsche wrote:

> *What!* Could mankind itself be in *decadence*? has it always been? — What is certain is that it has been *taught* only *decadence* values as supreme values. The morality of unselfing is the morality of decline *par excellence*, the fact 'I am perishing' translated

into the imperative 'you all *shall* perish' — and *not only* into the imperative! . . . The sole morality which has hitherto been taught, the morality of unselfing, betrays a will to the end, it *denies* the very foundations of life. — Let us here leave the possibility open that it is not mankind which is degenerating but only that parasitic species of man the *priest*, who with the aid of morality has lied himself up to being the determiner of mankind's values — who divines in Christian morality his means to *power* . . . And that is in fact *my* insight: the teachers, the leaders of mankind, theologians included, have also one and all been *decadents*: *thence* the revaluation of all values into the inimical to life, *thence* morality . . . *Definition of morality*: morality — the idiosyncrasy of *decadents* with the hidden intention of *revenging themselves on life* — and successfully. I set store by *this* definition. — (EH,132,133)

More than once Nietzsche referred to his Zarathustra as his "greatest gift to mankind." It may occur to those of his readers who are familiar with, and disciples of, his teachings, that in reading and experiencing his last book, *Ecce Homo*, this may be his greatest gift, his legacy, his final attempt and opportunity to be understood. Such a reader senses that Nietzsche himself fully grasped that this was the climactic event. It is sui generis, an astonishing, powerful, and beautiful performance.

Section Eight of "Why I Am A Destiny," reads:

Have I been understood? — I have not just now said a word I could not have said five years ago through the mouth of Zarathustra. — The *unmasking* of Christian morality is an event without equal, a real catastrophe. He who exposes it is a *force majeure*, a destiny — he breaks the history of mankind into two parts. One lives *before* him, one lives *after* him. . . The lightning-bolt of truth struck precisely that which formerly stood highest: he who grasps *what* was then destroyed had better see whether he has anything at all left in his hands. Everything hitherto called 'truth' is recognized as the most harmful, malicious, most subterranean form of the lie; the holy pretext of 'improving' mankind as the cunning to *suck out* life itself and to make it anaemic. Morality as *vampirism*. . . He who unmasks morality has therewith unmasked the valuelessness of all values which are or have been believed in; he no longer sees in the most revered, even *canonized* types of man anything venerable, he sees in them the *most* fateful kind of abortion, fateful *because they exercise fascination*. . . The concept

'God' invented as the antithetical concept to life — everything harmful, noxious, slanderous, the whole mortal enmity
against life brought into one terrible unity! The concept 'the
Beyond', 'real world' invented so as to deprive of value the *only*
world which exists — so as to leave over no goal, no reason,
no task for our earthly reality! The concept 'soul', 'spirit', finally even 'immortal soul', invented so as to despise the body,
so as to make it sick — 'holy' — so as to bring to all things in
life which deserve serious attention, the questions of nutriment, residence, cleanliness, weather, a horrifying frivolity!
Instead of health 'salvation of the soul' — which is to say a
folie circulaire between spasms of atonement and redemption
hysteria! The concept 'sin' invented together with the instrument of torture which goes with it, the concept of 'free will',
so as to confuse the instincts, so as to make mistrust of the
instincts into second nature! In the concept of the 'selfless',
of the 'self-denying' the actual badge of *decadence*, being *lured*
by the harmful, no longer being *able* to discover where one's
advantage lies, self-destruction, made the sign of value in general, made 'duty', 'holiness', the 'divine' in man! Finally — it
is the most fearful — in the concept of the *good* man common
cause made with everything weak, sick, ill-constituted, suffering from itself, all that *which ought to perish* — the law of *selection* crossed, an ideal made of opposition to the proud and
well-constituted, to the affirmative man, to the man certain of
the future and guaranteeing the future — the latter is henceforth called the *evil man* . . . And all this was believed in *as morality*! — *Ecrasez l'infâme*! — (EH,133,134)

In Section Nine, the last section of "Why I Am A Destiny," there
are eight words — question and answer, or question and riddle?
These are Nietzsche's words:

> — Have I been understood? — *Dionysos against the Crucified* . . .
> (EH,134)

Part Twelve

"Dionysos against the Crucified" . . . Nietzsche is a symbolist, a master in the art and practice, as well as the interpretation of symbols. Dionysos — the god, who in ancient religious ceremonies celebrated nature, *this life*, the human body, sexuality, procreation, birth, with music, dance, laughter, versus "the Crucified," the god, who in Christian religious ceremonies celebrates another world, *another life*, a spiritual rebirth, the human "soul." Two opposing symbols, two cultural signifiers. Nietzsche, assuming the mantle of the ancient god, would acclaim a recognition, a resurrection of the god — a recurrence of the joyful affirmation of nature, of this life, as opposed to the fictional suffering god of Christianity.

Humans share *one* common, natural world — the world which Nietzsche interpreted as a "monster of energy." Humans share *one* common life, one basic drive, one motive, which Nietzsche interpreted as "will to power." However, this natural world, shared by humans, is present in *two* types, or forms, of life — male bodies, experiences, "worlds," and female bodies, experiences, "worlds." Both types express power in creating and destroying. Humans create life, words or speech, values, and more. Nature is value-less and rank-less; creating values and creating ranking systems are human activities. We create the world which concerns humans.

This commonly shared natural world is present not only in two necessarily related human forms, female and male, but as dualistic throughout — the Logos of Heraclitus. Probably the pairs of opposites, other than the sexes, which Nietzsche wants to finally stress are those of truth and lie, affirmation and negation, and creativity and destruction.

The primary elements of Nietzsche's philosophy are nature, power, dualism, sexuality, values, and change — constituting the process of what it means to be human. Nietzsche's particular sense of change, not surprisingly, was to consider change as "to make or become different," and the stress was on *becoming*. We have followed him carefully in his detailed account of the process of becoming a single human being — himself. During this relatively short active lifetime of Nietzsche's, and his keen awareness of the changes continuing in himself, there were emerging also early signs of changes of a broader scope — cultural, intellectual, social changes. During this time, he became wise, clever, a writer of books. He also became a philologist, a philosopher, a psychologist, and a cultural critic and historian. As a product of his own German culture, and as a critic of that culture, he became a "destiny," a turning point in history.

Within the process of cultural history — German culture, and beyond that, Western culture — Nietzsche's deepening consciousness, his superior sensibilities, were functioning at their best. Doubts and questions were becoming impossible to disregard concerning the powers, the values, the honesty, the conflicts, the legitimacy, the authority — whether considerations were directed to human relations of class, of race, of nationality, of religion, or of sexuality. The right or status of a group supported by tradition, custom, religion, or accepted standards, or as conforming to recognized principles or accepted rules and standards, were increasingly becoming subjects for scrutiny. Equally threatening and disruptive were increasing challenges to authority — to the power to influence, to command or control thought, opinion, or behavior.

Remember these first words of the first chapter of *Ecce Homo*:

THE fortunateness of my existence, its uniqueness perhaps, lies in its fatality: to express it in the form of a riddle, as my father I have already died, as my mother I still live and grow old. This twofold origin, as it were from the highest and lowest rung of the ladder of life, at once *decadent* and *beginning* — this if anything explains that neutrality, that freedom from party in relation to the total problem of life which perhaps distinguishes me. I have a subtler sense for signs of ascent and decline than any man has ever had, I am the teacher *par excellence* in this matter — I know both, I am both. — My father died at the age of thirty-six: he was delicate, lovable and morbid, like a being destined to pay this world only a passing visit — a gracious reminder of life rather than life itself. (*EH*.38)

Nietzsche's "fatality" — its fortunateness and its uniqueness — from one of his perspectives, was that he was born October 15, 1844, a male child of a father who was a pastor, supposedly active within the Christian church, and a mother who was the daughter of a similar cleric. This was his personal, individual "fatality" — his "twofold origin."

From another of Nietzsche's perspectives, at the same time Nietzsche was born into a culture — German, European, Western — in which the doctrines of Christianity and the Christian church were beginning to undergo serious philosophical and theological critical challenges and opposition. This was his philosophical, cultural "fatality" — his other "twofold origin." Two parents, male and female — also two contexts, individual and cultural.

Nietzsche's father — "highest on the ladder of life," but participant in the declining and decaying institutions of Christianity — in Nietzsche's classification, a "decadent." As for his mother — "lowest on the ladder of life," she was apparently the symbolic (or literal) participant in the emerging, ascending, vaguely perceived new era.

Nietzsche's access to two experiences, two separate worlds — that of his male/father, the other of his female/mother — served to illuminate further his interpretations of the early stages of changes which could not be ignored. His "fatality" also meant that he would become an "agent of fate." Not a spectator, not a mere victim, but active, involved, engaged, in experiencing the inevitable outcome of the decay and destruction of Christianity, and the inevitable creation, or regeneration, of the next stage of Western culture. He was a decadent and its opposite. He would expose the self-destructive character of Christianity as it had become over centuries the dominant ideology of the West — driven by its morality of rank-relations of the power and value of males in relation to females. And he would contribute for future experimental developers many of the elements he thought necessary for what would involve momentous changes.

Nietzsche understands himself and his place in the battle. He is "dynamite." As to the future, his expectations are of unpredictable, unavoidable episodes, or events, of further increasingly violent destruction — "convulsions," "an earthquake spasm."

We know of Nietzsche's philological and philosophical studies, as well as his interests in cultural history. His perspectives reached far into the past, and played a critical role in his thinking. We know that he had insights into, and understanding of, himself and his present culture probably unequalled by any of his contemporaries. With his demand that philosophical thinking must become historical, as well as scientific, that meant that his own philosophical efforts to understand the process of human history must include the future. And, in projecting his sensibilities in that direction, his metaphors are as potent as ever. For individuals, there will be "convulsions" — "sudden, violent, spasmodic episodes of shaking, of contraction of the muscles, as of the body in a paroxysm." And for Western culture, an "earthquake spasm." "All the power-structures of the old society have been blown away."

From everything we heard from Nietzsche before he wrote these last few pages, we are fairly certain of the location of the center of the approaching earthquake. The pivotal point of power will be the power-structures involving males and females, with circles of damage to other power-structures radiating for great distances. Nietzsche believed that he was able to perceive, and interpret, the early signs of what appeared to predict the magnitude of such a future confrontation. His words, "there will be wars such as there have never yet been on earth. Only after me will there be *grand politics* on earth." "Grand," suggesting "inclusive, comprehensive, definitive, incontrovertible." Not petty politics, but global in scope and significance. And what, if not *sexual politics*? And, "politics," meaning "the use of intrigue and strategy to obtain a position of power." Or, maintain a position of power. Power and resistance to power. Nietzsche had been laying the groundwork for these later words almost from the beginning of his life.

Nietzsche sensed the early signs, or stages, of what he believed would become monumental changes. The millennia-long era of a cultural/world view which had its sources and maintenance in the experiences of the male/father — this "one-sided view" — was being recognized as no longer viable or sustainable. This era of dominance of the image of the father in Christianity, and of the male in society, was no longer tenable. The hierarchical model of male/female relations — relations of power and value — would inevitably evolve into some new model. And judging from Nietzsche's knowledge of the past and the present, the future would not evolve peaceably. On the contrary, Nietzsche sees a tumultuous period of integrating the "two worlds" — that of the female experience and that of the male experience.

The West, the world, would not remain monolithic. Reflecting Nietzsche's original principle, the cultural development would become, eventually and necessarily, again dualistic. In his interpretation, we could anticipate an approximation of a return to ancient, natural forms. Nietzsche left no doubt the direction which his own thinking was taking. Recall these words:

> *Revaluation of all values*: this is my formula for an act of supreme coming-to-oneself on the part of mankind which in me has become flesh and genius. (*EH*,126)

There is a process which I would call the "Nietzschean Revolution." Nietzsche took it upon himself to expose and destroy the antiquated system of values — Christian moral values, morality. And at the same time, he was beginning to assume leadership in the creation of a new and different system, or table of values. He reiterated many times that any culture is defined by its table of values. A change of the magnitude which Nietzsche was predicting was in the early stages — a "new moon," so to speak.

Recall again, Nietzsche's interpretation of the natural world, of nature, is that it is a "monster of energy." His interpretation of life, and especially of all human life, is that life is the "will to power." But in addition to that, life may be understood as meaning "a sequence of mental and physical experiences that make up the existence of an individual." As far as I am aware, Nietzsche was the first to affirm, and to include in all of his philosophical thinking, the very obvious fact that life is a continuing process of the experiences of two "worlds" — female experiences and male experiences.

Through his own experiences, Nietzsche became conscious of the fact that the foundation of human life resided in these two very different types of life experiences. This led to his affirming that it followed that males and females would have correspondingly different perspectives, different interpretations, different evaluations, different powers, different tastes, and more. The changes would involve the creation of new images, new meanings, new forms or models, and of course, new values — a revaluation of all values.

Nietzsche, as apparent "leader of the opposition," was already beginning to develop a plan, or strategy, to overturn the power-structures, and to prepare for the revaluation. In *Thus Spoke Zarathustra*, referring to his dictionary of symbols and images, he had written this:

> "Why so hard?" the kitchen coal once said to the diamond. "After all, are we not close kin?" Why so soft? O my brothers, thus I ask you: are you not after all my brothers?
>
> Why so soft, so pliant and yielding? Why is there so much denial, self-denial, in your hearts? So little destiny in your eyes?
>
> And if you do not want to be destinies and inexorable ones, how can you one day triumph with me?
>
> And if your hardness does not wish to flash and cut and cut through, how can you one day create with me?
>
> For creators are hard. And it must seem blessedness to you to impress your hand on millennia as on wax.
>
> Blessedness to write on the will of millennia as on bronze — harder than bronze, nobler than bronze. Only the noblest is altogether hard.

This new tablet, O my brothers, I place over you: *become hard!* (Z,214)

Hard and soft, male and female — and to the female, Zarathustra urges, "become hard." Together, and only together, female/mothers and male/fathers are able to create new life, or to create new values. This was Nietzsche's speaking of the future. The entire process of human life would be re-interpreted, rethought, re-appreciated, re-affirmed, revalued. I think he believed these changes were inevitable.

In *The Gay Science*, Nietzsche had written this:

> Someone took a youth to a sage and said: "Look, he is being corrupted by women." The sage shook his head and smiled. "It is men," said he "that corrupt women: and all the failings of women should be atoned by and improved in men. For it is man who creates for himself the image of woman, and woman forms herself according to this image."
>
> "You are too kindhearted about women," said one of those present; "you do not know them." The sage replied: "Will is the manner of men: willingness that of women. That is the law of the sexes — truly, a hard law for women. All of humanity is innocent of its existence; but women are doubly innocent. Who could have oil and kindness enough for them?"
>
> "Damn oil! Damn kindness!". Someone else shouted out of the crowd; "women need to be educated better!" — "Men need to be educated better," said the sage and beckoned to the youth to follow him. — The youth, however, did not follow him. (GS,126)

As for the creation of images, that prerogative had been in the possession of males for millennia. Old images — particularly of what it may mean to be a human male or a human female, would be re-thought, but not by males alone. Nietzsche had admonished the woman to "give birth to the overman." To the woman, he said, create a new image. And, Nietzsche had suggested several possibilities for the new image of the male. A favorite of mine reads:

> Not the strength but the permanence of superior sensibilities is the mark of the superior man. (BGE,74)

Thinking both backward and forward into history, Nietzsche announces:

> The more a woman is a woman the more she defends herself tooth and nail against rights in general: for the state of nature, the eternal *war* between the sexes puts her in a superior position by far. (*EH*,76)

In the process of life, or in the "production of the phenomenon we call 'life'," nature has placed the woman in a superior position. This is Nietzsche's "truth." Not in a higher *ranking* place, but nevertheless in a superior position. Nietzsche has been moving toward this explicit, simple statement since the opening words of *Ecce Homo*.

What was at stake was the necessity of abandoning the traditional, centuries-old interpretation of the cultural history of the West as a continuous process repeating a static, hierarchical, religiously-sanctioned order between the sexes — Christian morality — and creating a new interpretation, a new model or pattern. Given the long era of the antiquated, entrenched, and destructive sovereignty of Christian morality, it appears that Nietzsche foresaw for the future a comparable, turbulent, and perilous period of transformation.

Nietzsche's forecasting of convulsions and earthquakes yet to come within the changes which he believed were underway, were probably influenced in some important way by the presumed familiarity in his early years in Basel with the Swiss jurist, philologist, and cultural historian, J. J. Bachofen. After extensive scholarship in tracing and interpreting the cultural evolution of humans, Bachofen had determined that the evidence weighed heavily toward the view that human history could be understood as a series of stages of the continuing dynamics of power conflicts between males and females. And his impressions of these conflicts were graphic. He concluded:

> We shall come face to face with a new aspect of history. We shall encounter great transformations and upheavals which will throw a new light on the vicissitudes of human destiny. Every change in the relation between the sexes is attended by bloody events; peaceful and gradual change is far less frequent than violent upheavals. Carried to the extreme, every princi-

ple leads to the victory of its opposite; even abuse becomes a lever of progress; supreme triumph is the beginning of defeat. Nowhere is man's tendency to exceed the measure, his inability to sustain an unnatural level, so evident;. . . (MR,92,93)

Bachofen and Nietzsche were in agreement that changes of the magnitude each was perceiving — the changes involving the powers of males and females — had been the driving force of human history and would continue to be the dominant force. Looking into the future from his position and time, I believe Nietzsche considered what was beginning to emerge were changes in these powers and values unparalleled or unprecedented. As to the future, he expected a long period of mounting conflict before he could anticipate the achievement of his "revaluation of all values." In response to the incoming tide, the outgoing tide would not recede willfully, quietly, or peacefully.

PART THIRTEEN

Given the *intensity* of changes in the relations of power, whether of class, race, religion, nationality, or gender; given the *extensity* of these conflicts and changes; given the *momentum* of the development of events; and, given the *velocity* of these changes — during the 20th century and continuing into the 21st century — Nietzsche's forecast appears not to have been extravagant or ill-timed, but rather, evidence of his prescience. He *did* see himself as an "agent of fate."

Nietzsche foresaw that what the human community awaited was a new model of the process of life — a model jointly created, affirming both nature and culture; both female and male experiences; the dynamics of power, which recognizes the values and powers attached to creating life, preserving, protecting, defending, and enhancing life — a strategic dynamic harmony.

Three short passages — from among so many others — perhaps help in capturing the spirit of the legacy to which we are the heirs:

> *The ability to contradict.*—Everybody knows nowadays that the ability to accept criticism and contradictions is a sign of high culture. Some people actually realize that higher human beings desire and provoke contradictions in order to receive some hint about their own injustices of which they are as yet unaware. But the ability to contradict, the attainment of

a good conscience when one feels hostile to what is accustomed, traditional, and hallowed — that is still more excellent and constitutes what is really great, new, and amazing
in our culture: this is the step of steps of the liberated spirit:
Who knows that? (GS,239)

We who think and feel at the same time are those who really
continually *fashion* something that had not been there before:
the whole eternally growing world of valuations, colors, ac-
cents, perspectives, scales, affirmations, and negations. . . .
Whatever has *value* in our world now does not have value in
itself, according to its nature — nature is always value-less,
but has been *given* value at some time, as a present — and it
was *we* who gave and bestowed it. Only we have created the
world *that concerns man!* — But precisely this knowledge we
lack, and when we occasionally catch it for a fleeting moment
we always forget it again immediately; we fail to recognize
our best power and underestimate ourselves, the contem-
platives, just a little. We are *neither as proud nor as happy* as we
might be. (GS,241,242)

On the question of being understandable.—One does not only wish
to be understood when one writes; one wishes just as surely
not to be understood. It is not by any means necessarily an
objection to a book when anyone finds it impossible to understand: perhaps that was part of the author's intention — he
did not want to be understood by just "anybody." All the no-
bler spirits and tastes select their audience when they wish to
communicate; and choosing that, one at the same time erects
barriers against "the others." All the more subtle laws of any
style have their origin at this point: they at the same time keep
away, create a distance, forbid "entrances," understanding, as
said above — while they open the ears of those whose ears are
related to ours. (GS,343)

And finally, Nietzsche's vision of the future extended beyond the
continuing battle between "truth and the lie of millennia." From *Thus
Spoke Zarathustra*, which Nietzsche calls the "highest formula of affirmation which is attainable," here are three samples:

For *that man be delivered from revenge*, that is for me the bridge
to the highest hope, and a rainbow after long storms. (Z,99)

Whoever has gained wisdom concerning ancient origins will
eventually look for wells of the future and for new origins. O

my brothers, it will not be overlong before *new peoples* originate and new wells roar down into new depths. For earthquakes bury many wells and leave many languishing, but they also bring to light inner powers and secrets. Earthquakes reveal new wells. In earthquakes that strike ancient peoples, new wells break open.

And whoever shouts, "Behold, a well for many who are thirsty, a heart for many who are longing, a will for many instruments" — around that man there will gather a *people*, that is: many triers. (Z,211,212)

Thus I want man and woman: the one fit for war, the other fit to give birth, but both fit to dance with head and limbs. And we should consider every day lost on which we have not danced at least once. And we should call every truth false which was not accompanied by at least one laugh. (Z,210)

Conclusion

In the Introduction to this book, I suggested that Nietzsche believed that our world — our human world — always in the process of changing, would become something different and could become something better than it was, or is. And that what is required is changing the ways in which we perceive, feel, and think about this world. He developed strong positions on what such changes would entail, and proposed himself as an agent of these changes. That so many of his ideas, on which he actually staked the future, were radically original is evident.

In this book (as well as in two previous books) I have explored and sorted through many of the rich details of what appeared to reflect significant elements of the thinking of this exciting philosopher. The time has come to identify some major themes which are repeated with increased intensity, and variations, in all of Nietzsche's writings. These, it may be claimed, established his legacy, his gift of his very "personal property." They offer still new opportunities for further appreciation, interpretation, and evaluation. These ideas were transmitted by Nietzsche to future legatees. We have good evidence, and reasons, for considering these as the essential elements of what it means to be human — "all too human."

Nietzsche's thinking and writing, of course, reflected the scope of his scholarly and personal interests — philosophy, philology, physiology, psychology, science, art, music, poetry, religion, history, mythology, cultural criticism. He gave serious consideration to language, to words, often reflecting on such issues as his style, or styles, of writing; his obvious delight in playing with words, with devices such as riddles, puzzles, irony, or parables; his persuasion regarding the power of words, and of his own power, or ability, in such enterprises. He intended, believed, and demonstrated that his words were dangerous for his culture, at his time — and that they were difficult, while being magnetic and exciting. *How* to effect change, if not with words? And *who*, if not Nietzsche?

Nietzsche wrote in the German language, and he spoke of his own surprise that this language had been able to accommodate his very different and new uses. There is something else that confounds and amazes — rare, perhaps unique. He thought and wrote intermingling the language of mythos and the language of logos. That is, he was speaking simultaneously mythologically in the language of symbols, and philosophically, in so-called literal language. Think of symbolic as meaning "standing for, or suggesting, something else by reason of association, relationship, convention, or accidental resemblance." Think of literal as meaning "referring to the ordinary, primary meaning of a term." In his thinking and writing, Nietzsche gave new meaning to "bilingual."

Given that the range of Nietzsche's interests and learning was so extensive, it follows that the influences on his thinking were correspondingly numerous. Many of his literary predecessors provided significantly, and his roster and attributions are scattered throughout his writings. With his recognizing and crediting so many, nevertheless Nietzsche, I believe, establishes firmly the identity of his two favorites, the two protagonists in his dramatic philosophy — *Dionysus* and *Heraclitus* — Greek god of antiquity and Greek philosopher of antiquity.

Before making a final assessment of the significance of Nietzsche's devotion to both Dionysus and Heraclitus, first this. The task of possibly changing the world by changing the ways in which we perceive, and feel, and think about the world may be put in these terms. What needed to be done, what must be accomplished, was bringing humanity from the condition, or state, of unconsciousness to that of consciousness. It was imperative for humans to become aware of much that intentionally, or unintentionally, had been denied, ignored, concealed for centuries. It was sensibility that Nietzsche was speaking about, awareness of and responsiveness toward something — that something being *human experience.* Experience — individual and collective, natural and cultural. Experience, meaning "direct observation of, or participation in, events as a basis of knowledge." Experience, meaning "everything that is perceived, understood, remembered, both external and internal."

As we have discovered, Nietzsche made *his own experience,* or experiences, the primary source of his thinking and writing. I am suggesting that the recollected experiences of two relatively remote figures provided the original inspiration and life-blood which resulted in what Nietzsche considered his *becoming* wise and a writer of excellent books. These are Heraclitus and Dionysus.

Serving as a backdrop for looking more closely at Heraclitus, here these words from Nietzsche:

> The real philosophers of Greece are those before Socrates (— with Socrates something changes). They are all noble persons, setting themselves apart from people and state, traveled, serious to the point of somberness, with a slow glance, no strangers to state affairs and diplomacy. They anticipate all the great conceptions of things: they themselves represent these conceptions, they bring themselves into a system. Nothing gives a higher idea of the Greek spirit than this sudden fruitfulness in types, than this involuntary completeness in the erection of the great possibilities of the philosophical ideal. (WP,240)

> A few centuries hence, perhaps, one will judge that all German philosophy derives its real dignity from being a gradual reclamation of the soil of antiquity, and that all claims to "originality" must sound petty and ludicrous in relation to that higher claim of the Germans to have joined anew the bond that seemed to be broken, the bond with the Greeks, the hitherto highest type of man. Today we are again getting close to all those fundamental forms of world interpretation de-

vised by the Greek spirit through Anaximander, Heraclitus, Parmenides, Empedocles, Democritus, and Anaxagoras — we are growing more Greek by the day; at first, as is only fair, in concepts and evaluations, as Hellenizing ghosts, as it were: but one day, let us hope, also in our bodies! (WP,225,226)

Our contemporary way of thinking is to a great extent Heraclitean, Democritean, and Protagorean: it suffices to say it is Protagorean, because Protagoras represented a synthesis of Heraclitus and Democritus. (WP,233)

From among these so-called pre-Socratics, these earliest "scientific types of old philosophy," these philosophers of nature, Nietzsche gleaned the remnants of their various attempts to ascertain the essential, unifying, underlying material principle of unity in what they believed was an orderly universe. Perhaps water, or air, or earth, or atoms. According to Heraclitus — *fire*. The views of Heraclitus survive only as a few short fragments, attributed to him, and variously interpreted, by later philosophers. Looking back from Nietzsche's views to those of Heraclitus and then reversing that perspective, consider this possibility. From among the four substances, or elements — air, water, fire, and earth, formerly believed to compose the physical universe — fire presents the most immediate, intense, visible, volatile, force of *change*, of the *process* of something *becoming* something different. Perhaps this particular aspect of the physical world became for Heraclitus a kind of paradigm, or image, or metaphor used and expanded further in his account of the unity of the physical world.

We could expect that in adopting fire as the dominant focus in determining the basic unity of the natural world, Heraclitus would have been familiar with the rich symbolism which preceded him. For example, fire as an *image of energy*, associated with body-heat, spiritual energy, the agent of destruction and regeneration, of transformation, and many more meanings across many cultures. Or, the many associations with the Greek god, Prometheus. It appears that probably fire was the archetypal image of all natural phenomena.

In claiming to be a descendant and dedicated disciple of Heraclitus, Nietzsche was tracing his own rich, widely recognized, and enduring genealogy (even though both philosophers were unpopular, even scorned in their own time.)

The following is a passage of Nietzsche's written in 1885 and printed by the editors of *The Will to Power*:

> And do you know what "the world" is to me? Shall I show it to you in my mirror? This world: a monster of energy, without beginning, without end; a firm, iron magnitude of force that does not grow bigger or smaller, that does not expend itself but only transforms itself; as a whole, of unalterable size, a household without expenses or losses, but likewise without increase or income; enclosed by "nothingness" as by a boundary; not something blurry or wasted, not something endlessly extended, but set in a definite space as a definite force, and not a space that might be "empty" here or there, but rather as force throughout, as a play of forces and waves of forces, at the same time one and many, increasing here and at the same time decreasing there; a sea of forces flowing and rushing together, eternally changing, eternally flooding back, with tremendous years of recurrence, with an ebb and a flood of its forms; out of the simplest forms striving toward the most complex, out of the stillest, most rigid, coldest forms toward the hottest, most turbulent, most self-contradictory, and then again returning home to the simple out of this abundance, out of the play of contradictions back to the joy of concord, still affirming itself in this uniformity of its courses and its years, blessing itself as that which must return eternally as a becoming that knows no satiety, no disgust, no weariness: this, my *Dionysian* world of the eternally self-creating, the eternally self-destroying, this mystery world of the twofold voluptuous delight, my "beyond good and evil," without goal, unless the joy of the circle is itself a goal; without will, unless a ring feels good will toward itself — do you want a *name* for this world? A *solution* for all its riddles? A *light* for you, too, you best-concealed, strongest, most intrepid, most midnightly men? — *This world is the will to power — and nothing besides!* And you yourselves are also this will to power — and nothing besides! (*WP*,549,540)

R. J. Hollingdale included this passage in his book, *Nietzsche*, and suggests that although an unpublished note, it was of obvious significance to Nietzsche and enormously provocative and puzzling for his interpreters. If words are capable of arousing human consciousness of the experiences available of the awesome and mysterious world of nature, this single passage has that potential. In my view, it is power-ful and it is beautiful.

Thoroughly immersing himself in the "new" scientific environ-ment of his time, Nietzsche was himself conscious of the possibili-ties to be gained by listening to those "scientific types of old philoso-phy," those earlier philosophers of nature — Heraclitus in particular. While Heraclitus thought of *fire*, Nietzsche thought of *energy*. And he expressed this updated version in the vernacular of the science of his era — "monster of energy." But also as "this mystery world of the twofold voluptuous delight."

In addition to the influence of the Greeks, these few brief re-minders of modern science add to the emphasis that Nietzsche gave to energy. The first kind of energy to be recognized was the energy of motion, or kinetic energy, and all forms of energy are associated with motion. In 1853 in physics there was advanced the principle of "conservation of energy," stating that "the total energy of an isolated system remains constant irrespective of whatever internal changes may take place with energy disappearing in one form reappearing in another." In the 1840's it was conclusively shown that the notion of energy could be progressively extended to include forms other than kinetic energy.

In the passage quoted above, Nietzsche was extending the con-text of the principles of physics to cosmology, or the universe, and to humans — physiology, psychology, and culture. The passage is so meticulously wrought that is serves to communicate, or suggest, major elements of Nietzsche's thinking other than those associated directly with energy.

Heraclitus was important for the notion that fire forms the basic unifying principle of the natural universe, but further that the pro-cess of constant change results in a dynamic equilibrium maintaining an orderly balance in the world. This reflected the famous idea of the Logos, the formal pattern, or rationale. According to Heraclitus, en-ergy, motion, change, process, *and* pattern, form, regularity.

For Heraclitus, the image of fire functioned as his way of report-ing on the visibility of the constant, universal, process of change in the natural world, his principle of basic unity. Also, of equal consequence was his discovery, or recognition, of a more clearly defined sense of unity conveyed by sense experience. This was his notion of a Logos, a rationale permeating the entire universe — ubiquitous and eternal. For Heraclitus, this ordered, eternal pattern was understood as the *unity of pairs of opposites*. Pairs of opposites, necessarily interdependent, in a constant dynamic process of exchange and interchange, of equilibrium, tension, or conflict. This universe, made up entirely of opposites (this dualistic philosophy of nature), is the same common universe, shared by all humans, and is verifiable. It is both empirical and rational. In the thinking of Heraclitus, the monism of fire, change, process, upon elaboration apparently led to the idea of the dualism of opposites, or contraries. This primary contribution, the genius, of Heraclitus was in his apprehension of the formal unity of experience, the "uncanny dualism" which so fascinated Nietzsche.

And what of Dionysus, a nature god of ancient nature religions, a figure in the pantheon of Greek mythological gods and goddesses, before the beginning of philosophical speculation about the nature of things? Dionysus, also called Bacchus, especially associated with vegetation, wine, fruitfulness, ecstasy. The adoption of the Dionysian experiences, the Dionysian world, the Dionysian religion, is a theme that persisted from Nietzsche's first published book to the last. In some unpublished notes, he wrote:

> The word "*Dionysian*" means: an urge to unity, a reaching out beyond personality, the everyday, society, reality, across the abyss of transitoriness: a passionate-painful overflowing into darker, fuller, more floating states; an ecstatic affirmation of the total character of life as that which remains the same, just as powerful, just as blissful, through all change; the great pantheistic sharing of joy and sorrow that sanctifies and calls good even the most terrible and questionable qualities of life; the eternal will to procreation, to fruitfulness, to recurrence, the feeling of the necessary unity of creation and destruction. (*WP*,539)

> When the Greek body and the Greek soul "blossomed," and not in conditions of morbid exaltation and madness, there arose that mysterious symbol of the highest world-affirmation and transfiguration of existence that has yet been at-

tained on earth. Here we have a standard by which everything
that has grown up since is found too short, too poor, too narrow. One only needs to pronounce the word "Dionysus" in the
presence of Goethe, perhaps, or Beethoven, or Shakespeare,
or Raphael — at once we feel that our best things and moments have been *judged*. Dionysus is a *judge*! –Have I been understood? (*WP*,541)

Dionysus is considered, and used, by Nietzsche as a symbol of his
own experiences of, and responses to, the natural world. Dionysus,
the Dionysian religion, expresses the affective response — celebration, total affirmation of nature, life, the human body, sexuality, male
and female, unity, energy, powers. This lengthy passage expresses
vividly and dramatically Nietzsche's own view:

> I was the first to take seriously, for the understanding of the
> older, the still rich and even overflowing Hellenic instinct, that
> wonderful phenomenon which bears the name of Dionysus: it
> is explicable only in terms of an *excess* of force. Whoever fol-
> lowed the Greeks, like that most profound student of their
> culture in our time, Jacob Burckhardt in Basel, knew imme-
> diately that something had been accomplished thereby; and
> Burckhardt added a special section on this phenomenon to
> his *Civilization of the Greeks*. To see the opposite, one should
> look at the almost amusing poverty of instinct among the
> German philologists when they approach the Dionysian. The
> famous Lobeck, above all, crawled into this world of mysteri-
> ous states with all the venerable sureness of a worm dried up
> between books, and persuaded himself that it was scientific
> of him to be glib and childish to the point of nausea — and
> with the utmost erudition, Lobeck gave us to understand
> that all these curiosities really did not amount to anything.
> In fact, the priests could have told the participants in such
> orgies some not altogether worthless things; for example, that
> wine excites lust, that man can under certain circumstances
> live on fruit, that plants bloom in the spring and wilt in the
> fall. As regards the astonishing wealth of rites, symbols, and
> myths of an orgiastic origin, with which the ancient world
> is literally overrun, this gave Lobeck an opportunity to be-
> come still more ingenious. "The Greeks," he said (*Aglaophamus*
> I,672), "when they had nothing else to do, laughed, jumped,
> and ran around; or, since man sometimes feels that urge too,
> they sat down, cried, and lamented. *Others* came later on and
> sought some reason for this spectacular behavior; and thus
> there originated, as explanations for these customs, countless

traditions concerning feasts and myths. On the other hand, it was believed that this *droll ado*, which took place on the feast days after all, must also form a necessary part of the festival and therefore it was maintained as an indispensable feature of the religious service." This is contemptible prattle; a Lobeck simply cannot be taken seriously for a moment.

We have a different feeling when we examine the concept "Greek" which was developed by Winckelmann and Goethe, and find it incompatible with that element out of which Dionysian art grows — the orgiastic. Indeed I do not doubt that as a matter of principle Goethe excluded anything of the sort from the possibilities of the Greek soul. *Consequently Goethe did not understand the Greeks.* For it is only in the Dionysian mysteries, in the psychology of the Dionysian state, that the *basic fact* of the Hellenic instinct finds expression — its "will to life." What was it that the Hellene guaranteed himself by means of these mysteries? *Eternal* life, the eternal return of life; the future promised and hallowed in the past; the triumphant Yes to life beyond all death and change; *true* life as the over-all continuation of life through procreation, through the mysteries of sexuality. For the Greeks the *sexual* symbol was therefore the venerable symbol par excellence, the real profundity in the whole of ancient piety. Every single element in the act of procreation, of pregnancy, and of birth aroused the highest and most solemn feelings. In the doctrine of the mysteries, *pain* is pronounced holy: the pangs of the woman giving birth hallow all pain; all becoming and growing — all that guarantees a future — involves pain. That there may be the eternal joy of creating, that the will to life may eternally affirm itself, the agony of the woman giving birth *must* also be there eternally.

All this is meant by the word Dionysus: I know no higher symbolism than this *Greek* symbolism of the Dionysian festivals. Here the most profound instinct of life, that directed toward the future of life, the eternity of life, is experienced religiously — and the way to life, procreation, as the *holy* way. It was Christianity, with its *ressentiment* against life at the bottom of its heart, which first made something unclean of sexuality: it threw *filth* on the origin, on the presupposition of our life. (PN,560,561,562)

Earlier in a more sober voice and few words, Nietzsche had written:

What is astonishing about the religiosity of the ancient Greeks is the lavish abundance of gratitude that radiates from it. Only a very distinguished type of human being stands in *that* relation to nature and to life. Later, when the rabble came to rule in Greece, *fear* choked out religion and prepared the way for Christianity. (*BGE*,58)

And finally Nietzsche adds this:

Herewith I again stand on the soil out of which my intention, my *ability* grows — I, the last disciple of the philosopher Dionysus — I, the teacher of the eternal recurrence. (*PN*,563)

Dionysus became for Nietzsche the image and teacher of the direct observation, consciousness of, and participation in, "the phenomenon we call 'life'." It might be added that, according to the legends surrounding Dionysus and the religious rites in his honor, it appears that his converts and celebrants were mostly women. The men, however, we are reminded, responded with hostility.

Heraclitus, at a later date, from a different standpoint, and in a different voice — that of the philosopher — made clear, based on his own sense experiences, the orderly nature of the universe which the Dionysians had observed and worshipped earlier. And he became for Nietzsche the second voice, a constant presence in Nietzsche's life, and even more in his entire philosophical enterprise. Whereas Dionysus represented the *affective* response to nature, Heraclitus developed and expressed the *intellectual* response to the same natural orderly world.

Returning to these earliest sources of Western cultural tradition, Nietzsche developed what some would claim is the most dynamic, the richest, the most exciting philosophy perhaps ever — with perhaps the greatest potential for future discovery, exploration, and development. Although Nietzsche proclaimed his embrace of his Greek heritage, his thinking also clearly reflects his ties to his more immediate philosophical German predecessors, Immanuel Kant and G.W.F. Hegel. Additionally, he was fully engaged with the scientific and critical environment of his own time. However, he never failed to remind his readers (and to encourage them in a similar endeavor) that the ultimate source of his thinking was his own experience — and his unfailing and remarkable consciousness of that experience.

From Nietzsche we have learned — that to change our human world requires that we change the way, or ways, in which we perceive, or feel, and think about this world, which requires that we become conscious of certain important, even essential elements of our experience and of new possibilities of understanding these elements. Nietzsche would probably not have recognized, or accepted, any table ranking these numerous pieces in an order of significance. We can determine from his own writings, however, that these elements were constantly in play in human experience — interrelated and dynamic. And from his writings, in considering the idea of the *process of change* as central to all of his thinking, it becomes increasingly clear that in the human world, this process is bound inextricably to *power*. From one perspective, the point of reference for all of Nietzsche's ideas was the idea of power and the process of change involving power.

Just these reminders from Nietzsche regarding power. The world in its totality, and unity, is power — "a monster of energy." Life, as part of the world, is the will to power. Humans, as part of life, are also the will to power. The drive, or impulse, for power is the single motive of humans, defining all activities. The experience of power in humans is a feeling, a "generalized bodily consciousness." This feeling is experienced in either the activity of harming or the activity of benefiting — oneself or others. Life, or this feeling of power, he calls "good." The feeling of weakness he calls "bad." Happiness is defined as "the feeling that power is increasing." And, power is related inextricably to value, and is the basis of rank, or hierarchy, in the human world. Recall, in *Ecce Homo*, when Nietzsche casts his long perspective into the future, he says:

> The concept politics has then become completely absorbed into a war of spirits, all the power-structures of the old society have been blown into the air — they one and all reposed on the lie: there will be wars such as there have never been

on earth. Only after me will there be *grand politics* on earth.
(EH,127)

Politics understood as meaning "the art and use of intrigue and
strategies to obtain a position of power." Of many meanings, applications, contexts, expressions of the notion of energy, or power,
Nietzsche chose to focus on *human power* — as complicated as that is,
and as he has shown it to be.

Finally, we are able to make this claim. Nietzsche developed his
philosophy based on, or from, three basic principles, which together
serve as a kind of infrastructure. These three constitute the underlying foundation, or basic framework, of his thinking. They operate
continuously and together within the human world — natural and
cultural. These three are observable, universal, necessary, and eternal — constantly, variously, and repeatedly encountered. These principles, or phenomena, may be identified as *power, pattern,* and *process.*
Elaborated, first is the ambiguity and ubiquity of power; second, the
ordered pattern of opposites; and third, the ordered process of change.
Or, ubiquitous power, dualistic pattern, and dialectical process.

By dialectical process Nietzsche is reasserting Heraclitus' views
of the constant tension, or process, always occurring between two
opposites, interacting elements, or forces. Consider — the incoming
tide and the outgoing tide — one force becoming the opposite force,
and then reversal, "eternal recurrence." There are suggestions of a re-
latedness of correlation; of natural, reciprocal relations; of approxi-
mate equilibrium; of synergy, or mutually advantageous conjunction.
This is the Logos of Heraclitus. The consequences of the disruption
of this balance, or order, of disequilibrium — either by nature or by
humans — is violence.

Not cosmology, not the natural world in general, but recognizing
that *being human* is before all else, being part of this natural world —
something of a microcosm in relation to the macrocosm. And to give
full attention to understanding how these three principles apply to
our human situation. Nietzsche believed that in order to change the
human culture — with respect to beliefs, knowledge, behavior, social
structure, language, politics, religion, law, art, technology, and most

importantly, values — it was necessary to change the consciousness of human experience. With individuals, in words and images. To enable and urge individuals to *look* at what is being seen, to *listen* to what is being heard, to *think* and *speak* accordingly. Nietzsche appears to have excelled in his inexhaustible ability to create imaginative, vivid images.

We humans are a small part, a little world, a small unity, a miniature of the natural world. And that larger world? A unity of energy, of power. And as humans we constantly experience that energy, in *sensing* the external world and *feeling* the internal world. *Feeling the energy* — the generalized bodily consciousness or sensation — is direct and immediate; it belongs to the person; it is the dominant human impulse, or drive; it is what it means to be alive. We embody continuously energy or *power*. Look again at these brief words, written in 1872, and published posthumously:

> When one speaks of *humanity*, the idea is fundamental that this is something which separates and distinguishes man from nature. In reality, however, there is no such separation; "natural" qualities and those called truly "human" are inseparably grown together. Man in his highest and noblest capacities, is wholly nature and embodies its uncanny dual character. Those of his abilities which are terrifying and considered inhuman may even be the fertile soil out of which alone all humanity can grow in impulse, deed, and work. (PN,32)

Look again, too, at the following. In considering the possibility, or probability, that his readers were not alert, "awake," to this "uncanny dual character" — both of nature and of humanity, Nietzsche later wrote these words in *Beyond Good and Evil*, written and published in 1886:

> Everything deep loves masks; the deepest things have a veritable hatred of image and likeness. Might not *contrariety* be the only proper disguise to clothe the modesty of a god? A question worth asking. It would be surprising if some mystic hadn't at some time ventured upon it. There are events of such delicate nature that one would do well to bury them in gruffness and make them unrecognizable. . . Such a concealed one, who instinctively uses speech for silence and withholding,

and whose excuses for not communicating are inexhaustible, *wants* and encourages a mask of himself to wander about in the hearts and minds of his friends. And if he doesn't want it, one day his eyes will be opened to the fact that the mask is there anyway, and that it is good so. Every deep thinker needs a mask; even more, around every deep thinker a mask constantly grows, thanks to the continually wrong, i.e. superficial interpretations of his every word, his every step, his every sign of life.— (BGE,46,47)

Every human individual *embodies*, i.e. makes concrete and perceptible, both energy, or power, as well as this dualistic *pattern*. This pattern is observed in other so-called "microcosms," other individuals, and is observed and felt more directly and immediately in one's own body. One body, several functioning parts, two or each. Eyes, ears, hands, feet, arms, legs — left and right sides. Separate, opposite, interdependent, functioning together.

By the time that *Ecce Homo* was written in 1888, near the end of his productive life, Nietzsche's thinking was increasingly expanding, elaborating, and making explicit, these three ideas—*power, pattern,* and *process,* and the interplay among these in human experience. *Ecce Homo* is his final concerted climax, and the performance in which his interpretation of the principle of dialectical process is given its rightful recognition, and top billing. We have looked in detail at the wealth of Nietzsche's attention to the notion of change, or process — for him, more accurately expressed as *becoming.* To this book, Nietzsche gave the subtitle, "How One Becomes What One Is." And the entire book is his rendering of his intimate personal becoming, his life experiences, as the source and basis of his philosophy. Here Nietzsche is making his final and best attempt to increase the consciousness of his readers of the experience of being human — necessarily from *his* perspectives and interpretations. And, within the breadth and depth of his view, life is throughout a conglomerate of dialectical processes.

The scope of Nietzsche's perspectives and interpretations was given a narrower adaptation. From the most expansive, the natural universe, to life in general in that universe, to human life or persons in particular, to finally concentrate on the *human body.* Implicitly and explicitly, he had been insisting that the physical body and physiology was the starting point of knowledge, the primary object of concern, personal and philosophical. He was refocusing attention on understanding what it meant to become conscious of the total experience, to the body — the health of the body, the powers, the value, and much more.

We need to listen to Nietzsche's own words before proceeding further in this interpretation. Here are a few typical key passages:

> Everything that enters consciousness as "unity" is already tremendously complex: we always have only a semblance of unity.

> The phenomenon of the body is the richer, clearer, more tangible phenomenon: to be discussed first, methodologically, without coming to any decision about its ultimate significance. (WP,270)

> Essential: to start from the *body* and employ it as a guide. It is the much richer phenomenon, which allows of clearer observation. Belief in the body is better established than belief in the spirit. (WP,289)

> The unconscious disguise of physiological needs under the cloaks of the objective, ideal, purely spiritual goes to frightening lengths — and often I have asked myself whether, taking a large view, philosophy has not been merely an interpretation of the body and a *misunderstanding of the body*.

> Behind the highest value judgments that have hitherto guided the history of thought, there are concealed misunderstandings of the physical constitution — of individuals or classes or even whole races. All those bold insanities of metaphysics, especially answers to the question about the *value* of existence, may always be considered first of all as the symptoms of certain bodies. And if such world affirmations or world negations *tout court* lack any grain of significance when measured scientifically, they are the more valuable for the historian and psychologist as hints or symptoms of the body, of its success or failure, its plenitude, power, and autocracy in history, or of its frustration, weariness, impoverishment, its premonition of the end, its will to the end.

> I am still waiting for a philosophical *physician* in the exceptional sense of that word — one who has to pursue the prob-

lem of the total health of a people, time, race or of humanity — to muster the courage to push my suspicion to its limits and to risk the proposition: what was at stake in all philosophizing hitherto was not at all "truth" but something else — let us say, health, future, growth, power, life. (*GS*,34,35)

The evidence of the body.—Granted that the "soul" is an attractive and mysterious idea which philosophers have rightly abandoned only with reluctance — perhaps that which they have since learned to put in its place is even more attractive, even more mysterious. The human body, in which the most distant and most recent past of all organic development again becomes living and corporeal, through which and over and beyond which a tremendous inaudible stream seems to flow: the body is a more astonishing idea than the old "soul." (*WP*,347,348)

The three basic principles — power, contraries, and process — in numerous possible adaptations or permutations, appear to be solidly embedded in Nietzsche's thinking. His focus in thinking philosophically, as he insisted all philosophy should be, was on the meaning of being human, on what it means to exist as human. And that meant, first and always, to exist as the *body that you are*. He believed that the emerging sciences of medicine, physiology, and especially psychology, held unforeseen promise for understanding of the human body, and therefore human experience, in the future. Human physiology and the new psychology became for Nietzsche two additional major avenues in pursuing the understanding he was seeking. He was placing humans back into nature, and the human body-in-nature into philosophy — as central to philosophy.

In his becoming a philosopher — "a lover, or seeker, of wisdom" — Nietzsche was seriously involved from an early age in the possible meaning of wisdom. Not so much the questions "How do we acquire knowledge?" or, "What is called 'thinking'?", or "What is knowledge?", or many other similar questions. From an early age his quest was taking him into the past, to possible sources prior to the revered classical era of the Greeks, back to the ancients — as we have noted. As was his German predecessor, Hegel, Nietzsche was drawn irresistibly to the ideas of Heraclitus, and his understanding of wisdom has its sources in the thinking of Heraclitus. Perhaps a few of Heraclitus' own words are helpful:

> Those awake have one ordered universe in common, but in sleep every man turns to one of his own. (*PC*,18)

> Therefore it is necessary to follow the common; but although the Logos is common the many live as though they had a private understanding. (*PC*,18)

> Of the Logos, which is as I describe it, men always prove to be uncomprehending, both before they have heard it and when once they have heard it. For although all things happen according to this Logos men are like people of no experience, even when they experience such words and deeds as I explain, when I distinguish each thing according to its constitution and declare how it is; but the rest of man fail to notice what they do after they wake up just as they forget what they do when asleep. (*PC*,18)

> Sane thinking is the greatest virtue, and wisdom is speaking the truth and acting according to nature, paying heed. (*PC*,20)

> All men are granted what is needed for knowing oneself and sane thinking. (*PC*,20)

> Nature loves hiding. (*PC*,21)

"One ordered universe in common," "things of which there is seeing and hearing and perception" — this is the Logos of Heraclitus. This is the world of nature which Heraclitus described and interpreted. The Logos, often considered as immanent reason in the world; the principle of universal order; the active principle pervading and determining nature; the rationale or reason implicit in the universe, giving it form and meaning; cosmic, divine plan and process. And the human mind, the reasoning power in humans, is part of this natural plan and process. The Logos is the ultimate creative force, rules the universe, is divine or god-like.

More specifically, this Logos was described and interpreted by Heraclitus as a universe consisting wholly of pairs of opposites, each pair always unified by interdependence, and always in a state of constant conflict or competitive activity — a constant process of change, of "becoming." He describes this constant process as change in one direction ultimately balanced by corresponding change in the other direction — as a kind of dynamic equilibrium or orderly exchange of balance, like the pendulum. Neither one of any pair is the negation of the other. If the claims of only one of any pair are met, the result is destruction or injustice. It is unity which involves change, such as seasonal changes, or ocean tides. Heraclitus suggests fire as a symbol of this process of change — often rapid, creative, destructive. In Heraclitus' interpretation, as we saw, "wisdom is speaking the truth and acting according to nature" — understanding and following the Logos.

As to Dionysus, for Nietzsche this nature god became the dominating symbol of the ecstatic celebration of the powers and wonders of the natural world — the one Heraclitus would later describe as "one ordered universe in common." Dionysus, god of fruitfulness, vegetation, fertility, associated with wine and roses (symbolic of inspiration); god of trees and blossoming things, seasonal change, cyclic process, instinctive life, natural passions, the feminine.

In *Beyond Good and Evil*, in measured words, Nietzsche gives his interpretation of early nature religions, represented for him by the Dionysian religion. Again:

> What is astonishing about the religiosity of the ancient Greeks is the lavish abundance of gratitude that radiates from it. Only a very distinguished type of human being stands in *that* relation to nature and to life. Later, when the rabble came to rule in Greece, *fear* choked out religion and prepared the way for Christianity. (*BGE*,58)

And Nietzsche ended his *Ecce Homo* with these words:

— Have I been understood? — *Dionysus against the Crucified. .
. (EH,*134)

After carefully listening to Nietzsche's frequent accounts of
his revisiting with renewed appeal and applause the earliest of our
Western philosophers, and of his eagerness to re-establish his own
genetic identity with regard to these figures — as well as to their
antecedents — he successfully claimed his undeniable genealogy. He
was a descendant of Heraclitus, and proud of the relationship. That,
even though more than two thousand years separated the two.

For Nietzsche, the *natural world* is precisely as Heraclitus had
described and interpreted it. Also, Heraclitus' understanding of the
meaning of *human wisdom* was correspondingly the best. Heraclitus'
thinking, however, needed a timely restoration, or renewal. And
that updating was Nietzsche's self-appointed project. To the notion of "one ordered universe in common", Nietzsche added and/or
emphasized three aspects — *energy* or power, *sexuality,* and the *human
individual.*

From the new sciences, especially from physics, Nietzsche recognized the potential of the emerging interpretations of energy. And he
added these ideas to the Heraclitean version of the Logos, or the natural world. The world for Heraclitus in the 6th century B.C., expressed
in the image of fire, for Nietzsche in the 19th century expressed in the
image of "monster of energy." And remember, he names this world. It
is "the will to power." Energy, or power, defines the world, defines
life — it defines what it means to be human. Every living individual
is a microcosm, an embodiment of energy, of the will, or impulse, or
desire, for power. This will to power is a basic fact of life and of human experience.

Readers familiar with Nietzsche's writings know that his elaborations on this aspect of being human are limitless. The feeling of
power, the interpretation of power as the basic, single *motive* of all
human actions, the feeling of weakness and the effects of that feeling.
I have explored the idea of power throughout this book. Nietzsche's
philosophy of power is probably the most familiar of his many origi-

nal ideas. And, uses and abuses of his interpretations of the idea have contributed to many human disasters which have followed after him.

Nietzsche's ideas regarding power were alarming and generated consternation. But, he also raised the specter of *sexuality*. Nature, it appeared, was one ordered universe, grounded in energy, and universally and necessarily inhabited by female bodies and male bodies, in an ever recurring process called "life" — defined as the will to power. It also became clear that this pair of opposites, or contraries, stand out in nature as the original, the archetype of opposites. For the moment, enough said.

The detailed outlines of nature, of life, of humanity — observable and experienced ay *all* humans — had been persuasively drawn. Most philosophers before Nietzsche had addressed the question of the essential nature of *all* men, and had followed that interpretation by distinguishing and identifying men within groups — social, economic, political, religious, etc. From Plato's philosopher-kings, warriors, and artisans, to Hegel's customary citizens, courageous persons, victims and heroes, humans had typically been classified and categorized. Some were of one group, others of a different group.

Readers familiar with Nietzsche's writings also are aware of his emphasis on the single person — the *individual*. *All* humans share, participate in, and experience one ordered natural universe. *Some* humans in that natural world are in the group of males, *some* in the group of females. And especially, the experience of living in that natural ordered world is always as *one*, single human — an *individual*. The individual, as Nietzsche perceives the human community, is not a category, not an abstraction or concept. The individual is a separate, living individual female or a separate, living individual male. Both private and public — simultaneously one, some, and all. This is *who* you are, and what it means being human. One body, physiological and psychological, will to power throughout, constantly becoming *what* you are.

The exciting and mystifying qualities of Nietzsche's writings are to a large extent a result of his choice of a variety of forms, styles, and tones as means of speaking his "terrible truths," — those basic principles, ideas, wealth of interpretations. All of these forms were designed to convey to his readers the imprint — the indelible and per-

manent pattern and process of nature, the Logos. And also to awaken
these readers to the culture which had become superimposed on nature and on the identity of the readers themselves. Within his writings, Nietzsche considered *Zarathustra* his greatest, most profound
expression of the "meaning of wisdom."

Ecce Homo sounds very much as if Nietzsche was aware, and intended, that this was to become his final key signature to his tem-
pestuous adventures. To own, synthesize, and perhaps simplify those
many original insights and ideas. And so, he wrote a story — the story
of his life, of who he was and had become. Typically, "in the form of
a riddle." With dexterity and artistry, these insights and ideas, these
creations of his spent labor, became the motifs for the book which
Hollingdale values as "among the most beautiful books in German."

We have followed in much detail Nietzsche's personal story in
Ecce Homo. It is interesting to note that in *Beyond Good and Evil* he had
written this:

> Conversely, there is nothing impersonal whatever in the phi-
> losopher. And particularly his morality testifies decidedly and
> decisively as to *who he is* — that is, what order of rank the in-
> nermost desires of his nature occupy. (*BGE*,7)

The opening words of the first chapter of *Ecce Homo* serve as an
overture to the dramatic work which is developed. Remember:

> The fortunateness of my existence, its uniqueness perhaps,
> lies in its fatality: to express it in the form of a riddle, as my
> father I have already died, as my mother I still live and grow
> old. (*EH*,38)

This opening chord is followed immediately by "this twofold origin"; "this twofold succession of experiences"; "of apparently separate
worlds"; "the skill and knowledge to invert perspectives"; "life, the
great Yes to life". This last, the big "Yes", not from his father but from
his mother (the Dionysian yes). Nietzsche said "yes" to life, and to his
life, and lived his life accordingly — his "Amor Fati." A life proceed-

ing on the basis of unlimited and limited, necessary and contingent, responses of "yes" and "no."

The process of one particular individual life — Nietzsche's life — revealed as the embodiment of the world process of life, the Logos. And he leaves it to us to guess, or solve, his riddle. The entire story is uncanny. It suggests an association, or familiarity, with William Blake's "To see a world in a grain of sand."

Ecce Homo is Nietzsche's life story, his individual history, and his philosophy. It is another revelation of the observable universality of pairs of opposites constantly swirling throughout nature and life. It establishes unequivocally the prototypical status of sexuality — female/mother and male/father.

Throughout Nietzsche's writing one hears that the primary source of his thinking, and writing, was his own experiences, and his highly developed consciousness of those experiences. The implication is that this is the case with every individual person. Having devoted his life to thinking and writing at length about his ideas and insights, he chose in the end of his life to present these ideas and insights in this brief, relatively simple communication. The details of his "lived experience" is *Ecce Homo*.

Experience is always individual and unique. All humans live and share in common this one ordered natural world. In *Ecce Homo*, however, Nietzsche reminds the reader, and stresses, that the experience of this ordered universe is of two separate, very different forms —one male the other female. Within one shared world, "apparently separate worlds." Two sexes with correspondingly two different life experiences, and two consciousnesses of those experiences. This is his initial claim in *Ecce Homo*, and probably is his major interpretation of which he would urge others to become conscious.

I suggest the following. Nietzsche interprets the world — "a monster of energy," constantly "transforming itself." And as part of that world, life — "the will to power." As part of life, humans — "the will to power." As part of human life, two types — females and males. As part of this pair — one type, one individual, male or female. Before cultures add differences of race, class, religion, nationality, ethnicity, the individual, experiences, the consciousness of the individual experiences, is forever and naturally grounded in sexuality, or gender. *Same* world, *different* experiences — how Heraclitean, how Nietzschean.

Ecce Homo opens and closes with the dominant theme — sexuality, male and female, mother and father, the singular instance of opposites, archetype of all contraries. In this book Nietzsche gathers together many, perhaps most, of those ideas which had constantly and fully engaged his attention. The "real" world, energy or power, nature, life, the human body, perspectives, knowledge as interpretation, the senses, culture, history, criticism, religion, morality, speech, values. And. of course — contraries, sexuality, and change.

To the contraries male and female, in *Ecce Homo*, Nietzsche identifies a second pair of opposites — the affirmative "yes," and the negative "no." Together, these two pairs are the basic necessary factors determining the outcome of any single human life process. For every individual, your "facticity" — the state of being a fact, of actual human existence — and your "fatality" — established by fate, the inevitable outcome.

A person's sex or gender, and the ever present ability/necessity of indicating, or saying, yes or no, is the meaning of existing as a human person. In *Ecce Homo* Nietzsche says this:

> To accept oneself as a fate, not to desire oneself 'different' — in such conditions this is *great rationality* itself. (*EH*,47)

What it means to exist as a human being? To begin with, in the natural world, a person is a male and not a female, or a female and not a male — that is *who* you are; male or female, every person is one part of the pair of contraries consisting of both male and female. Natural, necessary, universal, observable. *What* any person becomes is the living process of affirming and negating, of saying yes or saying no. This dynamic is the process of change, or growth. It is the exercise of the will to power in every individual — the process of creating oneself. It is a major aspect of the Logos — the destructive and creative power of words.

Recall again. In reflecting upon his experiences, insofar as the relationship to his father and to his mother are significant to him, Nietzsche wrote:

> I regard it as a great privilege to have had such a father: it even seems to me that whatever else of privileges I possess is thereby explained — life, the great Yes to life, *not* included. (EH,42)

The original, final, ultimate yes is "the great Yes to life." And, his life-loving spirit of affirmation was the gift from his mother. Reporting on his observations, and his ability to observe, he wrote:

> To look from a morbid perspective towards *healthier* concepts and values, and again conversely to look down from the abundance and certainty of *rich* life into the secret labour of the instinct of *decadence* — that is what I have practised most, it has been my own particular field of experience, in this if in anything I am a master. I now have the skill and knowledge to *invert perspectives*: first reason why a 'revaluation of values' is perhaps possible at all to me alone. — (EH,39,40)

Taking both the perspective of his father and that of his mother, Nietzsche voiced his own "yes" to the perspective of the latter. As to his father, the advocate, or messenger, of the "no" of Christianity, Nietzsche had "already died." As to his mother, "I still live and grow old." This, too, from Nietzsche:

> This ultimate, joyfullest, boundlessly exuberant Yes to life is not only the highest insight, it is also the *profoundest*, the insight most strictly confirmed and maintained by truth and knowledge. (EH,80)

Considering both Nietzsche's philosophy and his personal life, I find it overwhelmingly persuasive to hear and acknowledge that in *Ecce Homo* his theme throughout is the contrast between those elements to which he spoke "yes" and those to which he spoke "no" — his *yeses* and his *noes*.

In no particular order, these are some of the important *yeses*: (1) the human body, that remarkable power-processing, power-converting organism; (2) power, as quantities of energy and abilities; (3) the self, self-affirmation, self-creation, self-respect, responsible selfishness; (4) the instincts; (5) the contraries; (6) little things, such as nutriment, recreation, the child; (7) speech, and the power of words; (8) "war," between the sexes, and of ideas and words; (9) change, or becoming — as of consciousness, of values, and of power relations; (10) new values; (11) two particular virtues — courage, meaning "mental or moral strength to venture, persevere, withstand danger, fear, or difficulty, or to resist opposition or hardship," and honesty, meaning "the refusal to lie, steal, or deceive."

Nietzsche's *noes* — the major, resounding, reverberating no-saying — were centered on Christianity. His attacks targeted especially the calamitous, ruinous effects on Western culture resulting from the spread over centuries of the power in establishing its morality — its hierarchy of ranking the value of the sexes. Exposing, and destroying, the lies, cruelty, and fears — what he saw as the viral anti-nature, anti-life values of Christianity — became Nietzsche's goal, his ultimate "No," He wrote:

> He who unmasks morality has therewith unmasked the valuelessness of all values which are or have been believed in; he no longer sees in the most revered, even *canonized* types of man anything venerable, he sees in them the most fateful kind of abortion, fateful *because they exercise fascination.* . . The concept 'God' invented as the antithetical concept to life — everything harmful, noxious, slanderous, the whole mortal enmity against life brought into one terrible unity! The concept 'the Beyond', 'the real world' invented so as to deprive of value the *only* world which exists — so as to leave over no goal, no reason, no task for our earthly reality! The concept 'soul', 'spirit', finally even 'immortal soul', invented so as to despise the body, so as to make it sick — 'holy' — so as to bring to all the things in life which deserve serious attention, the questions of nutriment, residence, cleanliness, weather, a horrifying frivolity! (*EH*,133)

Nietzsche's task, along with the goal of rejecting and changing the values of the Christian religion, was that of the "revaluation of all values." And he did exactly that in *Ecce Homo*, and in some of his earlier books, with his affirmations, his *yeses*. In his early years he had received his life-affirming spirit from his mother. In his later years he wrote:

> The more a woman is a woman the more she defends herself tooth and nail against rights in general: for the state of nature, the *war* between the sexes puts her in a superior position by far.— (EH,76)

In the *creative process of life*, Nietzsche reverses the centuries-old claim of the predominance of the male and assigns the superior place to the power and value of the female.

And finally *change*. Nietzsche was persuaded that in order to change the human world — contrary to the thinking of most of his predecessors — the change to be sought and effected involved changing the individual. Using one's powers to influence, affect the ways in which an individual sees, feels, and thinks about the world, nature, culture, life, oneself, and more. To change the consciousness of individuals, especially regarding power and values, and to emphasize the power of speech by humans to effect change. Words were/are the primary instrument of change — change which involves power and values. Looking into the future, the changes which Nietzsche articulated were changes of power-structures, or relations, and values — the basis of every culture.

Nietzsche was a philosophical revolutionary for his own time, and for ours. Yes, as he insisted, philosophy must become scientific, must become historical. But more importantly, the questions to be asked, the manner of framing the questions — and thereby the answers — must be revised and rethought. Such conventional considerations as the nature of man, mankind, the human species, and other similar abstractions, had become exhausted and ultimately irrelevant. No longer man, or the nature of man. Instead, human experience and consciousness of that experience, or those experiences. *And*, no longer would it be possible to ignore, or deny, the clearly evident, obvious fact that human experience was of two distinct, observable, and understandable forms — female experience and male experience.

BIBLIOGRAPHY

Nietzsche's Writings
(cited in the text by the initials given in parentheses)

Human, All Too Human (HA), Translated by Marion Faber, with Stephen Lehmann, Introduction and notes by Marion Faber (The University of Nebraska Press, 1984)

The Gay Science (GS), Translated, with Commentary by Walter Kaufmann (Vintage Books Edition, March 1974, Random House, Inc. 1974)

Thus Spoke Zarathustra (Z), Translated and with a Preface by Walter Kaufmann (The Viking Press, Inc., Compass Books Edition, 1966)

Beyond Good and Evil (BGE), Translated and with an Introduction by Marianne Cowan (Gateway Editions, Ltd., 1955)

Twilight of the Idols (PN), in *The Portable Nietzsche*, Selected and Translated, with an Introduction, Prefaces, and Notes, by Walter Kaufmann (The Viking Press, Inc., 1968)

The Antichrist (PN), in *The Portable Nietzsche*, Selected and Translated, with an Introduction, Prefaces, and Notes, by Walter Kaufmann (The Viking Press, Inc., 1968)

Ecce Homo (EH), Translated, with an Introduction and Notes, by R. J. Hollingdale, (Penguin Books, 1979)

The Portable Nietzsche (PN), Selected and Translated, with an Introduction, Prefaces, and Notes, by Walter Kaufmann (The Viking Press, Inc., 1968)

The Will to Power (WP), Translated by Walter Kaufmann and R. J. Hollingdale, Edited, with Commentary, by Walter Kufmann (Vintage Books Edition, 1968, Random House, Inc.)

Related Works

Nietzsche (N), by R. J. Hollingdale (first published in 1973 by Routledge & Kegan Paul Ltd.)

Myth, Religion, & Mother Right (MR), Selected Writings of J. J. Bachofen, Translated from the German by Ralph Manheim, with a Preface by George Boas and an Introduction by Joseph Campbell (published in 1967 by Princeton University Press, First Princeton/ Bollingen Paperback Printing, 1973)

Philosophic Classics (Thales to St. Thomas) (PC), by Walter Kaufmann (Prentice-Hall, 1961).

INDEX